PRACTICING MASS MEDIA RESEARCH

Study Guide for
Wimmer and Dominick's
Mass Media Research
S E C O N D   E D I T I O N

FRAN POWER JUDD
Surrey Consulting & Research, Inc.

■

ROGER D. WIMMER
Surrey Consulting & Research, Inc.

WADSWORTH PUBLISHING COMPANY
Belmont, California
A Division of Wadsworth, Inc.

© 1987 by Wadsworth, Inc. All rights reserved. No part of this book may be reproduced, stored in a retrieval system, or transcribed, in any form or by any means, electronic, mechanical, photocopying, recording, or otherwise, without the prior written permission of the publisher, Wadsworth Publishing Company, Belmont, California 94002, a division of Wadsworth, Inc.

ISBN 0-534-06705-0

Printed in the United States of America

1 2 3 4 5 6 7 8 9 10---91 90 89 88 87

CONTENTS

Preface v

Part One The Research Process 1

Chapter 1 Science and Research 3
Chapter 2 Research Procedures 15
Chapter 3 Elements of Research 31
Chapter 4 Sampling 47

Part Two Research Approaches 65

Chapter 5 Laboratory Research and Experimental Design 67
Chapter 6 Survey Research 83
Chapter 7 Field Research and Related Research Methods 103
Chapter 8 Content Analysis 117
Chapter 9 Longitudinal Research 139

Part Three Basic Statistics 155

Chapter 10 Introduction to Statistics 157
Chapter 11 Hypothesis Testing 175
Chapter 12 Inferential Statistics 187

Part Four Research Applications 201

Chapter 13 Research in the Print Media 203
Chapter 14 Research in the Electronic Media 219
Chapter 15 Research in Advertising and Public Relations 237
Chapter 16 Research in Media Effects 253

Part Five Analyzing and Reporting Data 265

Chapter 17 The Computer as a Research Tool 267
Chapter 18 Research Reporting, Ethics, and Financial Support 273

PREFACE

This study guide is designed to be used as a supplement to *Mass Media Research,* Second Edition, by Roger D. Wimmer and Joseph R. Dominick.

We strongly believe that completion of the exercises in the study guide, in conjunction with reading the text, will reinforce and enhance your learning about mass media research. The information covered in the study guide can also provide a valuable review for course exams.

The study guide is divided into five parts, which correspond to the five parts of the text. Chapters contain the following exercises:

> **Research Terms.** Space is provided for definitions that test your knowledge of significant mass media and research terminology presented in each chapter.
>
> **Review Questions.** Multiple-choice questions focus your attention on the major topics covered in each chapter and test your ability to recall and interpret mass media concepts, definitions, and facts.
>
> **Relational Definitions.** Short lists of terms or concepts pertaining to mass media are selected from the material covered in each chapter. By choosing the one term or concept that does not fit with the others, you will further refine your understanding of the material discussed in the text.
>
> **Concept Application Questions.** Specific mass media problems test your ability to generalize procedures and theories to practical research situations and to apply various research approaches.

Correct responses to the questions and problems in the study guide can be determined with a careful rereading of the text. For reference purposes, however, we have provided the pages in the text where correct responses can be found. These pages are indicated in parentheses after each research term, review question, and relational definition. (Page numbers are not provided for concept application questions, which require a broader, more detailed understanding of the material presented.)

PART ONE
The Research Process

1 SCIENCE AND RESEARCH

2 RESEARCH PROCEDURES

3 ELEMENTS OF RESEARCH

4 SAMPLING

CHAPTER 1
Science and Research

The mass media industry has come to rely on research for nearly every decision it makes. Researchers gather data that help management in corporate planning, data that are used to describe the media and how it develops, data that analyze how consumers use the medium for entertainment and information, and data that attempt to provide insight into how audiences are affected by radio, television, cable, and the print media.

In an effort to meet this increasing demand for media information, mass media researchers continue to develop methodologies for the collection of data and analysis of the role of media in society, as well as for the purpose of studying how media affect audience behavior. This effort has witnessed an important shift in the past several decades away from answers based on "gut feelings" and "common sense" and toward those based on scientific and more objective approaches, in other words toward what is measurable.

The purpose of Chapter 1 is to provide background on the development of mass media research and to discuss some of the methods used in collecting and analyzing media information, particularly from a quantitative perspective.

NAME _____

CLASS _____

DATE _____

RESEARCH TERMS

Use the space provided below to define the following terms.

1. Algorithm (3)

2. Applied research (13)

3. Constitutive definition (11)

4. Empiricism (10)

5. Operational definition (11)

6. Proposition (11)

7. Proprietary data (13)

8. Replication (10)

9. Scientific method (9)

10. Theory (11)

REVIEW QUESTIONS

Choose one response that best answers each question below.

1. Over the past 50 years, the most significant trend in mass media research has been (4)

    a. to increase media profits
    b. to study the effects of media on audiences
    c. to combine intuitive and scientific approaches
    d. to encourage cross-disciplinary studies
    e. c and d are correct

2. Historically, the first phase in the evolution of mass media research is concerned with (5)

    a. how media develop
    b. how people use the media
    c. media effects
    d. media's role in the marketplace
    e. policy making and the media

3. Which of the following has not been a direct contributor to the growth of mass media research? (6)

    a. the role of advertising dollars
    b. persuasion studies of mass media effects
    c. studies on violence and sexual content in the media
    d. the use of propaganda in World War I
    e. the baby boom

4. Of the various approaches used to answer research questions, which of the following has been most significant in mass media research? (9)

   a. belief in something as a trusted source
   b. reasoning based on what has happened in the past
   c. laboratory experiments conducted at universities
   d. the a priori method of thinking
   e. observing changes through a series of objective analyses

5. Research that uses the scientific method approach (9)

   a. focuses on the source of information
   b. gathers proprietary data
   c. is considered to be self-correcting
   d. is based on a combination of subjective and objective analysis
   e. is concerned with relating the present to the past

6. Replication is important in mass media research because (10)

   a. research ideas can be strictly defined and observed
   b. studies can be independently verified
   c. it allows for flexibility in classifying data
   d. it provides a basis for predicting behavior
   e. it corrects errors made in previous research

7. It is a common practice among researchers to keep raw research materials for (10)

   a. 1 year
   b. 5 years
   c. 7 years
   d. a period of time appropriate to the study
   e. it depends on whether the data are proprietary or public

8. The role of an operational definition in research is to (11)

   a. define a word by substituting other words for it
   b. separate ideas from concepts
   c. rule out eccentricities of judgment by researchers
   d. delineate procedures to be followed in experiencing and measuring a concept
   e. c and d are correct

9. An <u>objective measure</u> in scientific research (10)

    a. provides a clearly defined interpretation of a study's hypothesis
    b. is what is measured to eliminate errors
    c. is a statement that is in agreement with direct observation
    d. is any overt behavior pattern
    e. occurs when two or more independent observers can classify behavior in the same way

10. Which of the following statements is an example of an <u>constitutive definition</u>? (11)

    a. Ask your professor for the answer to Question 8.
    b. Students use paper and pens.
    c. A study guide is a book designed to recall learning.
    d. Pencils should be used to mark this study guide.
    e. a and d are correct

11. When researchers search for <u>patterns of uniformity</u> to explain data, they are developing (11)

    a. a hypothesis
    b. a proposition
    c. a theory
    d. possible variables
    e. a law

12. In mass media research, a theory is only as good as its ability to (11)

    a. relate the past to the present
    b. predict behavior
    c. successfully forecast a phenomenon or event
    d. explain patterns of uniformity
    e. define invariant relationships

RELATIONAL DEFINITIONS

In each example provided below, choose the one term or concept that does not fit with the others. Explain why.

1. trend data/image data/segmentation data/proprietary data (7)

2. tenacity/authority/empiricism/intuition (8)

3. systematic/critical/controlled/cumulative (8)

4. theory/proposition/law/variable (11)

5. private/replicable/objective/measurable/predictable (9)

6. propaganda/advertising/economy/violence (6)

CONCEPT APPLICATION QUESTIONS

1. Name at least three societal changes since World War I that have made mass media information based on hunches (and other less scientific conclusions) inadequate. What mass media research focus has developed out of each of these changes?

2. How has the media trend toward audience fragmentation influenced research methods used by mass media researchers?

3. A research company has been asked to conduct a study to determine the effectiveness of an antidrug commercial. To be considered "scientific," the research must include five basic characteristics. One is that the methodology used in the study must be replicable. What are the others?

4. Station WAAA in Anytown, U.S.A., is considering changing its format from album-oriented rock to easy-listening. This means station management will need to know how the demographics of the audience will change. Using the steps of the scientific method, explain how a researcher might approach this type of study.

5. A newspaper publisher has decided to merge with another publishing company that prints a rival daily in the same city. In order to plan for what will now become one newspaper, the publisher wants to know what image the public has of both newspapers individually. What would the publisher take into consideration before deciding whether to hire a researcher at the state university or a private research company to conduct this study? Why?

CHAPTER 2
Research Procedures

Two basic tenets of mass media research are that (1) the process of evaluating a problem must follow a sequence of carefully defined scientific steps and (2) singular research findings provide only an <u>indication</u> of what may or may not exist. Since mass media research analyzes questions about human behavior, particularly human communicative behavior, at best it is a blend of insight into human nature and the desire to investigate observations through objective analysis.

Mass media research, like any other form of "objective" inquiry, adheres to a prescribed set of steps with the goal of eliminating as much error as possible. In order for a research study to be considered reliable and valid, as well as contribute to the understanding of mass media in general, it is crucial that researchers rigorously gather and analyze data so that they can be understood and replicated by others. And the results of a study must allow researchers to generalize their findings to larger audiences.

Chapter 2 focuses on how mass media problems are approached using the scientific method. How are research topics selected? When is a topic considered relevant? How can a perceived problem be stated as a "workable" research question? What considerations are crucial in developing a research design? And, once data have been collected, how must they be analyzed and interpreted so that the findings are considered to measure the problem researchers initially set out to understand?

NAME _____

CLASS _____

DATE _____

<u>RESEARCH TERMS</u>

Use the space provided below to define the following terms.

1. Artifact (34)

2. Control group (36)

3. Cross-validation (37)

4. Data archive(s) (22)

5. Demand characteristics (artifact) (37)

6. Design-specific results/sample-specific results/method-specific results (39)

7. Double blind experiment (37)

8. Evaluation apprehension (37)

9. Experimental design (30)

10. Experimenter bias (37)

11. External validity (27)

12. Field service (32)

13. History (artifact) (35)

14. Hypothesis (29)

15. Instrument decay (36)

16. Internal validity (34)

17. Literal replication/operational replication/
    instrumental replication/constructive replication (39)

18. Maturation (artifact) (35)

19. Mortality (36)

20. Pilot study (32)

21. Point of prior equivalency (36)

22. Research design (30)

23. Research question (29)

24. Secondary analysis (22)

25. Selection (artifact) (37)

26. Statistical regression (artifact) (36)

27. Testing (artifact) (36)

REVIEW QUESTIONS

Choose one response that best answers each question below.

1. Research conducted scientifically (18)

    a. eliminates the possibility of error
    b. results in data that are externally valid
    c. increases the likelihood of producing relevant data
    d. reduces the need for duplication of studies
    e. a and c are correct

2. The research approach of secondary analysis enables researchers (22)

    a. to evaluate otherwise unavailable data
    b. to save time and resources
    c. to detect errors or misinterpretations
    d. to use already proven data
    e. a and b are correct

3. Which of the following can be considered a <u>disadvantage</u> of secondary analysis of research data? (23)

   a. data are usually difficult to access
   b. data can be reanalyzed
   c. studies often do not include enough information about scientific procedures
   d. investigations are limited because the original design cannot be altered
   e. c and d are correct

4. The difference between a <u>hypothesis</u> and a <u>research question</u> is (29)

   a. a research question provides indications about variable relationships
   b. a hypothesis is used to develop research questions
   c. a research question is used to gather preliminary data
   d. a hypothesis is a testable statement
   e. a and d are correct

5. To ensure that a research design produces <u>reliable and valid</u> results, a researcher must (31)

   a. assess long-term effects on subjects
   b. analyze phenomena in a single session if possible
   c. exclude normal intervening variables
   d. eliminate spurious intervening independent and dependent variable relationships
   e. a and d are correct

6. A <u>research artifact</u> (34)

   a. allows researchers to explain similarities in research findings
   b. indicates a lack of external validity in a study
   c. shows that a study has succeeded in investigating its hypothesis
   d. is a variable that creates a rival explanation of results
   e. c and d are correct

7. Which of the following is not an example of an artifact? (35-37)

    a. fatigue
    b. memorization of interviewer questions
    c. a high school drop-out
    d. outdated equipment
    e. respondent's need to please

8. Cross-validation enables researchers to (37)

    a. rule out statistical regression
    b. prevent mortality in a study
    c. test for homogeneity of subjects
    d. spot discrepant results
    e. b and d are correct

9. Evaluation apprehension occurs when (37)

    a. subjects are aware of the purpose of a study
    b. subjects want to be accepted by other subjects
    c. subjects attempt to confound their responses
    d. subjects respond passively to researchers' questions
    e. b and d are correct

10. Double blind experiments allow researchers to (37)

    a. know whether a subject belongs to an experimental group or a control group
    b. prevent observational bias
    c. reduce experimenter bias
    d. b and c are correct
    e. a and c are correct

11. Which of the following is not used by researchers to increase external validity in a study? (38)

    a. replication of a study
    b. use of homogeneous samples
    c. use of random samples
    d. lengthening the period of time in which the study is conducted
    e. all of the above are used

12. Which of the following cannot be used to help validate a scientific test? (39)

   a. duplication of the sampling procedures used
   b. duplication of the experimental procedures used in a previous study
   c. variation of the experimental conditions of the original study
   d. avoiding imitation of previous studies
   e. using subjects with similar characteristics

13. Studies that use <u>instrumental replication</u> (39)

   a. duplicate the dependent measures used in a previous study
   b. eliminate previous research error
   c. vary methods of statistical analysis
   d. alter the research design
   e. c and d are correct

RELATIONAL DEFINITIONS

In each example provided below, choose the <u>one</u> term or concept that does not fit with the others. Explain why.

1. problem selection/research review/replication/hypothesis statement (19)

2. research design/data collection/theory review/data analysis (19)

3. hypothetical/testable/tentative/preliminary (29)

4. control/research/laboratory/experimental design (30)

5. naturalistic/realistic/unobtrusive/confounding (31)

6. rival explanations/internal validity/extraneous variable/maturation (34)

7. history/maturation/external validity/mortality (35)

8. heterogeneous sample/multiple exposures/random sample/control group (38)

9. scientific fact/design-specific/replicable/reliable (39)

10. operational/literal/experimental/instrumental (39)

CONCEPT APPLICATION QUESTIONS

1. Researchers have been asked by a cable TV company to determine whether its programming of college courses for credit is meeting the needs of its adult viewing audience. What kinds of questions will the researchers need to ask to determine if the study is feasible?

2. Using the example in Question 1, identify a hypothesis or research question the researchers might seek to answer once they have determined that the study has merit.

3. What four characteristics of research design must the researchers consider to ensure that the study in Question 1 will produce reliable and valid results?

4. Ten artifacts are commonly encountered in research design. For each of the ten, give an example of an artifact that might appear in the study described in Question 1.

5. Again referring to Question 1, what three procedures might the researchers use to ensure that the study for the cable TV company is externally valid? Why is this important?

6. Why is replication of research imperative before the results of a particular study can be said to be significant?

CHAPTER 3
Elements of Research

In nearly everything we do, we form theories--ideas about why things are the way they are. These ideas allow us to explain and predict our world. Scientific theories, however, are not drawn out of the air: they are developed in particular and definable steps.

Scientific research is empirical--that is, researchers must be able to <u>perceive</u>, <u>classify</u>, and <u>measure</u> information that relates to the question they are attempting to analyze.

Chapter 3 discusses three basic characteristics of scientific inquiry that researchers must understand before they can develop theories about mass media communication. These elements include <u>concepts</u> and <u>constructs</u>, <u>variables</u>, and <u>measurement</u>.

First, researchers develop ideas about mass media based either on what they observe or on more ambiguous thoughts: these ideas are called <u>concepts</u>. In this process, researchers consider how their ideas or observations might be related, and they then look for patterns and general explanations.

Once researchers have an area of investigation in mind, they bring a group of observations together with the goal of studying these in an objective manner. With this information, they make <u>constructs</u>, or inferences, about audience behavior.

Finally, Chapter 3 discusses how researchers <u>measure</u>, or quantify, the data they have collected. Concepts and constructs are believed to exist because of some cause or causes, which can be defined by more than one element. These elements are called <u>variables</u> and are phenomena that can be measured or manipulated. Measurement, then, is the process of assigning numbers to the data according to specific rules.

NAME   _____

CLASS   _____

DATE   _____

RESEARCH TERMS

Use the space provided below to define the following terms.

1. Antecedent variable (47)

2. Concept (45)

3. Concurrent validity (63)

4. Construct (45)

5. Construct validity (63)

6. Continuous variable (57)

7. Control variable (47)

33

8. Criterion variable (47)

9. Dependent variable (46)

10. Discrete variable (57)

11. Dummy variable (54)

12. Equivalence (55)

13. Face validity (62)

14. Independent variable (46)

15. Index (57)

16. Intercoder reliability (60)

17. Isomorphism (52)

18. Marker variable (46)

19. Measurement (51)

20. Multivariate analysis (46)

21. Nominal level/ordinal level/interval level/ratio level (53-56)

22. Predictive validity (63)

23. Qualitative research (49)

24. Quantitative research (50)

25. Reliability (59)

26. Scale (57)

27. Semantic differential (58)

28. Stability (61)

29. Test-retest method (61)

30. Triangulation (51)

31. Validity (62)

32. Variable (46)

REVIEW QUESTIONS

Choose one response that best answers each question below.

1. A concept is formed by (45)

    a. inferences from previous studies
    b. combining several hypotheses
    c. the process of eliminating theories
    d. noticing relationships between observations
    e. summarizing from generalities to particulars

2. Which of the following is not an example of a concept? (45)

    a. love
    b. readability
    c. banana
    d. athletic ability
    e. none of the above

3. Concepts are important in mass media research because they (45)

    a. allow researchers to eliminate unnecessary data
    b. enable researchers to organize "patterns" and form explanations
    c. provide a common interpretation of ideas
    d. let researchers measure related behavior patterns
    e. b and c are correct

4. A construct in mass media research (45)

    a. must be observed over time to be considered useful
    b. is determined as a result of testing
    c. permits specificity in definitions of behavior patterns
    d. is created for a particular scientific purpose
    e. c and d are correct

5. In all types of research, variables (46)

    a. are used to relate concepts
    b. are manipulated by researchers to develop constructs
    c. are used by researchers to eliminate false hypotheses
    d. are ambiguous and difficult to measure
    e. b and c are correct

6. Independent and dependent variables are different because (46)

   a. an independent variable cannot be measured
   b. an independent variable is manipulated and observed while a dependent variable is not
   c. an independent variable is manipulated, while a dependent variable is observed for effects
   d. the value of an independent variable depends on a dependent variable, but not vice versa
   e. c and d are correct

7. In nonexperimental research, an independent variable is known as (47)

   a. a criterion variable
   b. an antecedent variable
   c. a marker variable
   d. a dummy variable
   e. a and b are correct

8. Control variables are often used to (47)

   a. explain marker variables
   b. eliminate "noise" or unwanted influences in a study
   c. ensure that results of a study are due to dependent variables
   d. divide constructs into specific categories
   e. b and d are correct

9. An operational definition (48)

   a. is more crucial for measurable variables than dependent variables
   b. forces researchers to describe specific results in generalities
   c. indicates sources of potential error in a study
   d. explains how a variable will be manipulated but not measured
   e. none of the above

10. <u>Qualitative research</u> can be said to (49)

    a. eliminate the artificial quality of experimental studies
    b. be more flexible but more difficult to generalize from
    c. allow for greater objectivity in research studies
    d. have little use in gathering preliminary research data
    e. a and b are correct

11. <u>Quantitative research</u> can be said to (50)

    a. be more reliable and usually less time consuming than qualitative research
    b. often result in a loss of objectivity
    c. communicate results in numbers
    d. be concerned with how often variables are present
    e. c and d are correct

12. <u>Measurement</u> in mass media research (51)

    a. allows researchers to know the degree of similarity between what is studied and what exists in reality
    b. quantifies indications of the properties of individuals or objects
    c. is based on the implicit quantitative meaning of numbers
    d. calls for carefully explicated measurement techniques
    e. b and d are correct

13. At which level of measurement do numbers have <u>no</u> mathematical significance? (53)

    a. nominal
    b. ordinal
    c. interval
    d. ratio
    e. isomorphic

14. Which form of measurement <u>does not</u> rank data along some <u>dimension</u>? (55)

    a. ordinal
    b. nominal
    c. interval
    d. ratio
    e. b and d are correct

15. The difference between a discrete variable and a continuous variable is (57)

    a. a continuous variable cannot be divided into smaller subsections
    b. a continuous variable can take on any value and a discrete variable cannot
    c. a discrete variable can only include a whole unit of measurement
    d. a discrete variable is used more often in mass media research
    e. b and c are correct

16. The difference between a scale and an index is (57)

    a. indexes are based on more than one variable
    b. scales are not used in single- or two-item measurements
    c. scales have formalized rules for developing single indicators
    d. a and c are correct
    e. none of the above

17. Before a study incorporates the use of a scale or an index, researchers should (59)

    a. eliminate all but one theory
    b. conduct several studies to ensure reliability and validity
    c. narrow the variables being measured to five or less
    d. test previously validated measurements
    e. none of the above

18. A measure is said to be reliable if (59)

    a. at different times, the measure provides identical data
    b. the measure provides different answers over short intervals but is consistent over longer periods of time
    c. results in no error
    d. can be used to detect relationships between variables
    e. a and d are correct

19. <u>Intercoder reliability</u> occurs when (60)

   a. observers use similar operational definitions but not particularly the same measuring instrument
   b. researchers hold similar perceptions of what is being measured
   c. results of a study can be achieved by other observers
   d. results of a study can be achieved consistently over time
   e. measures show internal consistency

20. Problems with <u>stability</u> in research result when (61)

   a. results of a study are inconsistent over time
   b. procedures are not operationally defined
   c. there is a time lag between subsequent testing
   d. results of a study are inconclusive
   e. a and b are correct

21. The <u>test-retest method</u> of determining reliability (61)

   a. measures the degree of equivalence in a study
   b. uses correlation coefficients to determine stability
   c. measures the consistency of results
   d. scores test results with different measurement techniques
   e. b and c are correct

22. Assessing <u>validity</u> in measurement depends on (62)

   a. judgment on the part of the researcher
   b. evaluating degrees of congruence between a variable's operational and conceptual definitions
   c. whether or not a study measures what it is supposed to
   d. a and c are correct
   e. all of the above

23. When researchers check the measuring instrument they are using <u>against some present criterion</u>, they are searching for (63)

   a. construct validity
   b. face validity
   c. concurrent validity
   d. predictive validity
   e. equivalent validity

RELATIONAL DEFINITIONS

In each example provided below, choose the one term or concept that does not fit with the others. Explain why.

1. summarizing/abstract idea/related observations/inferences (45)

2. conventionalism/authoritarianism/chair/superstition (45)

3. phenomenon/manipulation/measurement/concept (46)

4. independent/operational/marker/antecedent (46)

5. predictor variable/control variable/noise/relevant categories (47)

6. clear statement/measure/relevant variables/data analysis (48)

7. case study/field observation/focus group/laboratory study (49)

8. precision/measured/numbers/triangulation (54)

9. numerals/rules/isomorphism/assignment (51)

10. nominal/ratio/scale/interval (53)

11. ranked/equivalent/exhaustive/mutually exclusive (54)

12. rank/dummy variable/equivalence/equal intervals (55)

13. true zero point/intervals/parameters/scale (56)

14. subsections/discrete/infinite values/height (57)

15. Likert/Roman/semantic differential/bipolar scale (58)

16. true score/low ratio/random error/ambiguous wording (60)

17. validity/intercoder reliability/equivalence/stability (60)

CONCEPT APPLICATION QUESTIONS

1. A fashion magazine publisher wants to determine readership acceptance of two different cover designs being considered as a change for the publication. Design a possible research approach that might be used to conduct this study. Identify the following items as they would apply to the study you have designed.

    a. Independent variable(s)

    b. Dependent variable(s)

    c. Type of measurement(s)

    d. Controls for reliability and validity

2. A researcher is involved in a project to test the design of a new syndicated TV show. The producers are interested in viewer reactions to the show's opening (titles, graphics, music), set design, host, and overall show concept. The researcher designs a series of measurement instruments, conducts the study with a randomly selected group of viewers, and presents the results to the producers. With respect to reliability and validity, what problems may result from this approach?

CHAPTER 4
Sampling

Although mass media research requires the objective analysis of specific communication questions, subjects studied must allow researchers to make predictions about their behavior that can be generalized to larger populations. Conducting a census in which every member of a population is studied is in most cases impractical, if not impossible. Thus, researchers most often analyze <u>random samples</u> of populations and use their findings to make predictions about other groups.

Since results taken from a portion of a population are used to generalize, researchers must be certain that the methods they use to select a sample are both reliable and valid.

Chapter 4 describes two basic types of samples commonly used in mass media research: <u>probability samples</u> and <u>nonprobability samples</u>. Within these two broad categories of sampling there are many subcategories used by researchers to select subjects used in studies.

This chapter also discusses problems inherent in determining sample size, as well as methods used to reduce the possibility of sampling error.

NAME _____

CLASS _____

DATE _____

RESEARCH TERMS

Use the space provided below to define the following terms.

1. Available sample (71)

2. Census (69)

3. Cluster sampling (77)

4. Confidence interval (83)

5. Confidence level (83)

6. Homogeneity (76)

7. Incidence (76)

8. Measurement error (69)

9. Multistage sampling (78)

10. Multivariate study (81)

11. Nonprobability sample (70)

12. Parameter (70)

13. Periodicity (76)

14. Population (69)

15. Probability sample (70)

16. Psychographics (85)

17. Purposive sample (72)

18. Quota sample (72)

19. Random digit dialing (73)

20. Random error (82)

21. Random sample (73)

22. Rating (82)

23. Sample (69)

24. Sample weighting (85)

25. Sampling error (69)

26. Sampling frame (75)

27. Sampling interval (75)

28. Sampling rate (75)

29. Stratified sample (76)

30. Systematic sampling (75)

31. Volunteer sample (72)

REVIEW QUESTIONS

Choose one response that best answers each question below.

1. A sample that is adequate for testing purposes (69)

   a. tests most members of a population
   b. cannot, in most cases, be generalized
   c. is representative of an entire population
   d. is free of measurement error
   e. results in measurement error but not sampling error

2. A <u>probability sample</u> (70)

    a. does not follow guidelines of mathematical probability
    b. allows researchers to calculate sampling error
    c. does not incorporate the use of systematic selection
    d. collects exploratory data for designing measurement instruments
    e. most often relies on the use of available samples

3. The use of an <u>available sample</u> is controversial because (71)

    a. voluntary subjects are used
    b. it is not a representative sample
    c. it contains unknown quantities of error
    d. it has no internal validity
    e. b and c are correct

4. A <u>volunteer sample</u> (72)

    a. is a form of probability sampling
    b. can be more easily generalized to entire populations
    c. can significantly bias the results of a research study
    d. may lead to inaccurate estimates of population parameters
    e. c and d are correct

5. A <u>purposive sample</u> (72)

    a. eliminates subjects who fail to meet specific criteria
    b. is representative of the general population
    c. is selected to meet a predetermined percentage of a population
    d. includes subjects who possess higher educational levels
    e. a and d are correct

6. The use of <u>random sampling</u> allows researchers to (73)

    a. select subjects who seem to meet specific requirements
    b. reduce sampling error
    c. provide all subjects with an equal chance of selection
    d. use a subject again for another study
    e. c and d are correct

7. A disadvantage of a simple random sample is (75)

   a. researchers cannot statistically determine external validity
   b. elimination of the possibility of classification error
   c. subjects cannot be used for other studies
   d. sampling error tends to be higher compared to other sampling procedures
   e. subjects do not have an equal chance of being selected

8. Systematic sampling results in (75)

   a. greater accuracy because sampling frames are used
   b. savings of time and money
   c. easy sample selection
   d. preventing periodicity from biasing a study
   e. b and c are correct

9. Researchers use the method of stratified sampling when (76)

   a. a representative group of subjects is readily available
   b. subjects with a specific trait are tested
   c. a study needs to be done in a short period of time
   d. the rate of incidence in a study is low
   e. a and b are correct

10. Incidence in a study describes (76)

    a. how often particular types of subjects are used
    b. the frequency with which desired subjects can be/are found
    c. the use of several stratified variables
    d. when time and expense for recruiting are low
    e. b and d are correct

11. Cluster sampling creates problems for researchers because (77)

    a. comparisons cannot be made to other populations
    b. a higher rate of error in sample selection is common
    c. a complete list of the population is necessary
    d. population clusters are rarely clearly defined
    e. b and d are correct

12. Multistage sampling is a form of (78)

    a. stratified sampling
    b. random sampling
    c. cluster sampling
    d. nonprobability sampling
    e. c and d are correct

13. In determining sample size for a research study, researchers are most concerned with (81)

    a. economic constraints of a study
    b. the methodology to be used in the study
    c. subject mortality
    d. selecting a larger sample than is required
    e. all of the above

14. Research error is comprised of (82)

    a. random error and standard error
    b. standard error and measurement error
    c. random error and measurement error
    d. sampling error and measurement error
    e. sampling, measurement, and random error

15. Confidence levels in sampling errors (83)

    a. are ensured by calculating standard error
    b. relate to the degree of variance in values
    c. indicate how often a particular result will occur
    d. provide an indication of the degree of accuracy in a research study
    e. b and c are correct

16. Sample weighting in research is often necessary because (85)

    a. ideal population samples are impossible to obtain
    b. of time and expense constraints
    c. samples must be balanced to be valid
    d. it reduces the possibility of error
    e. all of the above

RELATIONAL DEFINITIONS

In each example provided below, choose the one term or concept that does not fit with the others. Explain why.

1. population/census/sample/concept (69)

2. replication/cost/time constraints/study purpose (71)

3. random tables/representative sample/systematic selection/ mathematical guidelines (70)

4. available sample/volunteer sample/purposive sample/unknown error (71)

5. systematic sampling/order of items/bias/homogeneous groups (76)

6. sample categories/multistage sampling/representative sample/ reduced costs (77)

7. significant variable/heterogeneous groups/subsample/incidence (76)

CONCEPT APPLICATION QUESTIONS

1. The publishers of a large newspaper want to determine whether or not its readers like the concept of daily contests. What four considerations would researchers need to address before deciding whether to use a probability sample versus a nonprobability sample?

2. Suppose you are in an introductory mass media class and you and your classmates are asked to participate in a study that will help researchers design a questionnaire to determine the amount of violence contained in MTV videos. What arguments for and against using an "available sample" will the researchers need to consider?

3. Researchers are conducting a study to determine the likelihood of persons with annual incomes over $25,000 purchasing a cellular mobile telephone in the next 6 months. They plan to use the method of systematic sampling. How might they acquire a sample population? What problems might they encounter?

4. <u>Popular Science Magazine</u> wants to use a cluster sample to determine how much the general public understands about nuclear fission. What two potential sources of error will they need to consider?

5. Name four general principles researchers should follow to determine sample size.

6. Fifty people volunteered to participate in a study to determine the effects of rapid editing (quick cuts between scenes) in music videos on feelings of anxiety and nervousness. What will researchers need to consider to eliminate the possibility of bias created by volunteer subjects?

7. In a study to measure the difference between color quality and picture clarity on five television sets made by different manufacturers, would researchers be more likely to use a purposive sample or a quota sample? Why?

8. Researchers plan to conduct a telephone survey to determine what listeners think of a particular radio station's DJs. What method might they use to ensure that a random sample is obtained? Why? In this case, would the rate of incidence be high or low? Why?

9. A researcher wants to generate a simple random sample to analyze readership of 15 out of a total of 100 popular magazines. Explain how Table 4.1 on page 74 of your text can be used, and then generate 15 numbers from the table. Explain your procedure.

10. A study using a random sample of 900 newspaper readers shows that only 10% of the readers read the editorial page on a daily basis. Referring to the formula for calculating standard error on page 82 of your text, determine the amount of standard error for this study. What would the range for the actual percentage of readers be?

PART TWO
Research Approaches

5 LABORATORY RESEARCH AND EXPERIMENTAL DESIGN
·
6 SURVEY RESEARCH
·
7 FIELD RESEARCH AND RELATED RESEARCH METHODS
·
8 CONTENT ANALYSIS
·
9 LONGITUDINAL RESEARCH

CHAPTER 5
Laboratory Research and Experimental Design

Because the mass media are complex in variety and usage, researchers must use a number of different research approaches to investigate media questions. Chapter 5 focuses on the role of one approach in particular--<u>laboratory research</u>.

Laboratory experiments, which have been a staple of mass media research for several decades, offer several advantages to mass media researchers: they follow a relatively simple format, and the relationships among variables can be measured under closely observed and controlled conditions.

The blueprint for researchers who use the laboratory methodology is called the <u>experimental design</u>. This process provides the steps the researcher will follow to accept or reject a hypothesis or research question. Sometimes this process is quite simple. Other times the experimental design will involve many different groups and numerous treatments.

The laboratory research approach has shortcomings, as do all research procedures, but the method has proved efficient in many instances and will continue to be used by mass media researchers.

NAME _____

CLASS _____

DATE _____

RESEARCH TERMS

Use the space provided below to define the following terms.

1. Environmental artificiality (90)

2. Environmental control (90)

3. Experimental design (92)

4. Factor (95)

5. Factorial designs (95)

6. Laboratory method (89)

7. Latin Square design (93)

8. Panel design (93)

9. Posttest-only control group (94)

10. Pretest-posttest control group (93)

11. Repeated measures design (93)

12. Solomon four-group design (94)

13. Subject control (91)

14. t-test (94)

15. Variable control (91)

REVIEW QUESTIONS

Choose <u>one</u> response that best answers each question below.

1. The <u>laboratory method</u> of mass media research (90)

    a. allows researchers to study attitudes but not causation
    b. permits isolating a testing situation
    c. often generates invalid or irrelevant media data
    d. is used only for preliminary analyses of problems
    e. b and c are correct

2. Laboratory research does <u>not</u> give researchers control over (90)

    a. rival explanation of results
    b. confounding influences
    c. internal validity
    d. external validity
    e. types of dependent variables

3. <u>Control</u> in experimentation is important because (91)

    a. studies with fewer variables are more reliable
    b. there is less opportunity for multiple results
    c. experimental artificiality is ruled out
    d. research questions are more valid
    e. none of the above

4. An <u>advantage</u> of controlling the number of variables is (91)

    a. a reduction in the number of subjects needed
    b. elimination of confounding influences
    c. strengthened internal validity
    d. less need for greater numbers of experimental groups
    e. b and c are correct

5. An <u>experimental design</u> consists of (92)

    a. construction of a measurement instrument
    b. the order of laboratory research
    c. assignment of subject to groups
    d. identification of independent variables
    e. b and d are correct

6. In which of the following studies would researchers be likely to use a repeated measures design? (93)

   a. the effect of cartoons on children's anxiety level between the ages of 3-6
   b. liking/nonliking of local radio personalities
   c. people's attitudes toward a newspaper's layout
   d. opinions about a cable network's Sunday programming
   e. all of the above

7. The major difference between a pretest-posttest and posttest-only is (93-94)

   a. in a posttest-only, each group faces the same variables in the study
   b. in a pretest-posttest, subjects are not randomly selected
   c. in a posttest-only, at least three groups are required
   d. in a pretest-posttest, both groups are tested before the experimental treatment is given
   e. a posttest-only considers the aspect of external validity

8. Which type of experimental design would most likely be used to study whether or not people are more likely to purchase a product after they have been exposed to a commercial? (93)

   a. pretest-posttest
   b. pretest
   c. Latin Square
   d. repeated measures
   e. posttest-only

9. An advantage of using the pretest-posttest control group design is (93)

   a. subjects all face the same circumstances in the study
   b. fewer subjects are required
   c. fewer experiments are necessary
   d. there is greater control over artifacts
   e. a and d are correct

10. The desire to avoid _____ causes researchers to use a <u>posttest-only</u> control group. (94)

    a. using a t-test
    b. exposing a treatment variable
    c. rival explanations
    d. subject sensitization to the test
    e. c and d are correct

11. A <u>t-test</u> is used to determine (94)

    a. subject sensitization to a posttest
    b. whether experimental groups are affected by artifacts
    c. whether a significant statistical difference is present
    d. reasons for rival explanations
    e. whether a pretest might be a negative factor

12. The <u>Solomon four-group design</u> (94)

    a. determines effects and interaction of testing
    b. considers the aspect of external validity
    c. allows for greater generalizability than a posttest-only
    d. is useful if a pretest design alone is undesirable
    e. all of the above

13. A <u>factorial design</u>, unlike a simple randomized design, (95)

    a. accounts for interaction between independent variables
    b. cannot measure more than three variables
    c. tests differences between groups for statistical significance
    d. is more reliable than pretest-posttest designs
    e. analyzes the need to have a number of factors

14. The concept of <u>levels</u> in factorial design refers to (95)

    a. manipulation of two or more factors
    b. simultaneous testing of independent variables
    c. measurement of more than one variable at a time
    d. a 2 x 2 x 2 factorial design
    e. all of the above

15. A study to compare attitudes of two groups <u>before</u> and <u>after</u> an experimental treatment has been given is (93)

   a. a factorial design
   b. a pretest-posttest group design
   c. a Solomon four-group design
   d. a posttest group design
   e. b and c are correct

16. An experimental design that indicates the following order is (94)

$$\begin{array}{ccc} R & X & O_1 \\ R & X & O_2 \end{array}$$

   a. a two-factor design
   b. a Solomon four-group design
   c. a pretest-posttest control group
   d. a repeated measures design
   e. a posttest-only control group

17. In the example in Question 16, if two more groups were added and given a pretest, the diagram would describe a (94)

   a. Solomon four-group design
   b. four-factor design
   c. pretest group design
   d. panel study
   e. none of the above

18. Researchers want to know if male and female college students are more likely to use a study guide, classroom notes, or cassette tapes to supplement a textbook. Which type of experimental design would they be most likely to use? (96)

   a. a 2 x 2 x 2 factorial design
   b. a 2 x 3 factorial design
   c. a pretest-posttest group design
   d. either b or c
   e. none of the above

19. A radio station wants to know whether a billboard advertising campaign or poster ads on public transportation had more influence in getting listeners to tune into their new station. Which <u>experimental method</u> would a researcher most likely use? (95)

   a. a telephone survey
   b. a pretest-posttest group design
   c. a repeated measures design
   d. either a or c
   e. a 2 x 2 factorial design

RELATIONAL DEFINITIONS

In each example below, choose the <u>one</u> term or concept that does not fit with the others. Explain why.

1. environment/subjects/variables/manipulation (89)

2. selection/assignment/mortality/experimental treatment (91)

3. experimental treatment/posttest/survey/pretest (92)

4. random group assignment/observation/measurement/factor (92)

5. pretest/control of rival explanations/t-test/subject sensitization (94)

6. interaction/simultaneous analysis/independent variables/ posttest-only (95)

7. experimental design/sample selection/factor/data analysis (97)

CONCEPT APPLICATION QUESTIONS

1. List the five basic uses of the laboratory approach in mass media research.

2. Name two mass media studies that would require researchers to use a laboratory approach. Why would this approach be preferable over less controlled conditions?

3. A researcher decides to use the laboratory approach to study whether or not rhetoric in political campaigns affects voter preference. What argument(s) might critics of the experimental method in mass media research use to discredit such a study?

4. In the example in Question 3, what elements might the researcher control to strengthen the internal validity of the study?

5. Using the Campbell and Stanley notations on page 92 of your text to represent parts of an experimental design, outline a study to determine the effects of MTV on record sales in your hometown.

6. Researchers want to determine whether the residents of a large metropolitan area are more likely to change their driving habits as a result of a "clean air" campaign heard on the radio or seen on TV commercials. Design an experiment to address this issue.

7. List the advantages/disadvantages of the four types of experiments listed below:

Pretest-posttest control group:

Latin Square design:

Posttest-only control group:

Solomon four-group design:

Factorial design:

CHAPTER 6
Survey Research

The use of surveys in mass media research has been a popular and widely used method of data collection for decades. The increased use of the survey methodology, however, has created changes in the way surveys are conducted and reported. More attention is now given to sample selection, questionnaire design, and error rates.

Chapter 6 discusses the advantages and disadvantages of using survey research, as well as the steps researchers use in conducting this methodology.

Researchers can select from several types of survey approaches: <u>mail</u>, <u>telephone</u>, <u>personal interview</u>, and <u>group administration</u>. The type of survey used will often depend on the purpose of the study, the amount of time available to the researcher, and the amount of money allocated for the study.

A researcher who decides to use the method of survey research must follow a number of prescribed steps. These include defining the purpose of the study, deciding whether to use a <u>descriptive</u> or <u>analytical</u> approach, designing a questionnaire, and selecting a sample. The methods used to analyze data collected by a survey are also discussed in this chapter.

NAME _____

CLASS _____

DATE _____

RESEARCH TERMS

Use the space provided below to define the following terms.

1. Analytical survey (102)

2. Close-ended question (106)

3. Descriptive survey (102)

4. Dichotomous response (110)

5. Double-barreled question (108)

6. Feeling thermometer (113)

7. Filter question (107)

8. Forced-choice question (112)

9. Leading question (108)

10. Mailing list (120)

11. Mutually exclusive response (110)

12. Open-ended question (105)

13. Prestige bias (132)

14. Rating scale (111)

15. Response ratio (130)

16. Semantic differential scale (111)

17. Structured interview (127)

18. Unstructured interview (127)

REVIEW QUESTIONS

Choose one response that best answers each question below.

1. The difference between a descriptive and an analytical survey is (102)

   a. descriptive surveys describe possible situations
   b. analytical surveys examine interrelationships of variables
   c. analytical surveys draw explanatory inferences
   d. descriptive surveys document why situations exist
   e. b and c are correct

2. An advantage of survey research over laboratory research is (103)

   a. survey research can determine causality
   b. increased reliability and validity
   c. the absence of artificiality in testing
   d. survey research can manipulate many independent variables
   e. c and d are correct

3. The first step in designing a survey questionnaire should be to (104)

   a. design unambiguous questions
   b. determine the type of data collection method to be used
   c. decide whether to ask close or open-ended questions
   d. determine the goals of the study
   e. decide whether or not to do a pilot study

4. A significant problem in <u>questionnaire design</u> is how to (104)

   a. determine the proper length of a questionnaire
   b. avoid biasing effects
   c. determine the reliability of questions asked
   d. ask single questions that will measure complex concepts
   e. avoid sensitive and personal questions

5. A <u>successful</u> survey question should always (105)

   a. require respondents to generate their own answers
   b. communicate clearly and unambiguously
   c. provide information that can be used in pilot studies
   d. allow researchers to detect hidden meanings in responses
   e. none of the above

6. <u>Close-ended questions</u> provide researchers with (106)

   a. a number of response alternatives
   b. preliminary data for a pilot study
   c. greater uniformity of responses
   d. flexibility to translate data into numbers
   e. c and d are correct

7. Questionnaires using <u>close-ended questions</u> must (106)

   a. compensate for a lack of variety of responses
   b. be somewhat ambiguous to obtain a "feeling" response
   c. allow some overlap in answer categories
   d. indicate intensity of positive and/or negative responses
   e. a and d are correct

8. The simplest type of <u>close-ended question</u> is a (110)

   a. forced-choice question
   b. multiple-choice question
   c. dichotomous response
   d. mutually exclusive question
   e. rank-ordered question

9. To compensate for the <u>disadvantages</u> of using close-ended questions, a survey using this method should (106)

   a. permit grouping answers into categories for content analysis
   b. include a number of filter questions
   c. include the opportunity for an unanticipated response
   d. use double-barreled questions for more in-depth responses
   e. a and c are correct

10. A disadvantage of using an <u>open-ended question</u> is (106)

    a. there is greater likelihood of experimenter bias
    b. responses are too varied to be of much help in designing pilot studies
    c. researchers cannot determine why respondents answer as they do
    d. content must be analyzed before it can be tabulated
    e. the likelihood of uniformity of responses

11. A potential for <u>positive or negative bias</u> in a survey is created by (108)

    a. using proper names in the survey
    b. lack of parsimony in a survey
    c. asking sensitive or personal questions
    d. reliance on open-ended questions
    e. a and c are correct

12. Regarding the <u>order</u> in which questions should be asked on a questionnaire, it is common that researchers (116)

    a. ask close-ended questions before open-ended questions
    b. ask personal/demographic questions first, then issue-related questions
    c. proceed from the general to the specific
    d. use preliminary questions to generate subject interest in the study
    e. c and d are correct

13. Which question below can be defined as <u>double barreled</u>? (108)

    a. Some people think some sex education should be taught in the schools. Do you favor more or less sex education, or none at all?
    b. Do you favor reducing the number of illegitimate births by teaching sex education in the schools?
    c. _____ Sex education is necessary to stop illegitimate births.
       _____ Sex education will increase the number of illegitimate births.
    d. Do you favor sex education in the schools?
       ___Yes   ___No
       (If yes, go to Question 5)   (If no, skip Question 5)
    e. Like most Americans, do you believe sex education should be taught at home rather than in the schools?

14. An <u>advantage</u> of using the mail-survey technique is (120)

    a. reasonable cost
    b. elimination of interviewer bias
    c. anonymity
    d. the ability to gather data from any geographic area
    e. all of the above

15. Which of the following elements of mail-survey questionnaire design would likely have the greatest <u>negative</u> influence on the rate of response? (116)

    a. question contamination
    b. short version versus long version
    c. asking demographic questions at the beginning of the questionnaire
    d. telling the respondents how much time will be involved
    e. c and d are correct

16. The most significant <u>disadvantage</u> of a mail survey is (122)

    a. the need for questions to be self-explanatory
    b. the need to cover a wide geographic area
    c. the slow return rate
    d. the low return rate
    e. a and c are correct

17. Which of the techniques below is the most common way to increase the rate of response to a mail survey? (122)

    a. keeping the questionnaire to one page or less
    b. following up with a letter from 3-4 weeks after the initial mailing of the survey
    c. using monetary inducements
    d. asking for subjective rather than objective information
    e. all of the above

18. An advantage of using a telephone survey over a mail survey is (123)

    a. it is generally less expensive
    b. it results in higher response rates
    c. respondents are not influenced by interviewers
    d. types of questions asked are less limited
    e. b and d are correct

19. The difference between a structured and unstructured interview is (127)

    a. structured interviews ask open-ended questions followed by close-ended questions
    b. structured interviews ask questions in a predetermined order
    c. unstructured interviews do not allow respondents freedom to respond
    d. structured interviews are more difficult to tabulate
    e. b and d are correct

20. The largest single drawback to personal interviews is (129)

    a. interviewer bias
    b. cost
    c. developing rapport
    d. skepticism among interviewees
    e. the perception that the study is sanctioned by some authority

21. Response rate in survey research refers to the (130)

    a. percentage of respondents chosen to participate in a survey
    b. number of people sampled divided by the number who refused
    c. lack of availability of respondents
    d. number of people interviewed divided by number of people sampled
    e. percentage of response from a specific group

22. Which of the following is not considered in the response ratio calculation? (131)

    a. everyone who did or did not respond
    b. respondents or units screened out
    c. disconnected phone numbers
    d. surveys returned with incomplete data
    e. b and c are correct

23. The completion rate is highest for which of the following survey methods? (131)

    a. face-to-face interviews
    b. personal interviews
    c. mail surveys
    d. telephone interviews
    e. a and b are correct

24. Biasing in response rate patterns is not affected by (131)

    a. one sex responding more than the other
    b. lack of responses from a specific population group
    c. information from secondary sources
    d. underrepresentation of respondents
    e. uncooperative respondents

25. Which survey method would researchers most likely use to determine how people's beliefs changed after they viewed a TV series on euthanasia? (102)

    a. analytical survey
    b. feeling thermometer
    c. descriptive survey
    d. focus group
    e. none of the above

26. A private research company plans to use a telephone survey to determine what listeners aged 18-34 think of the morning DJs on several local radio stations. The greatest <u>advantage</u> of this method would be (123)

   a. it offers more control and a greater response rate
   b. it is less expensive than a mail survey
   c. it can be done without a pilot study
   d. sampling errors are eliminated
   e. a and d are correct

RELATIONAL DEFINITIONS

In each example below, choose the <u>one</u> term or concept that does not fit with the others. Explain why.

1. description/documentation/attitudes/variables (102)

2. variable interrelationships/document conditions/ explanation/description (102)

3. realistic setting/low cost/multiple variables/causality (103)

4. open ended/filter/forced/dichotomous response (105)

5. ambiguous/double barreled/multiple choice/leading (107)

6. standardized questions/predetermined order/broad questions/ restrictive interviewing (127)

CONCEPT APPLICATION QUESTIONS

1. As a researcher, you have been asked to design a survey to measure the viability of an all-sports format on an FM station in a large metropolitan area. Identify four major advantages of using a survey over other research methods to investigate this question.

2. Using the example in Question 1, identify three major disadvantages of using the survey method. What might the researchers do to correct or eliminate these problems?

3. Describe three studies for which researchers might use a descriptive survey. How could the purpose of these surveys be changed to require an analytical survey approach?

4. Below are open-ended questions that might appear in a survey questionnaire. Rewrite each question so that it becomes a close-ended question. What are the advantages and disadvantages of both types of questions?

   a. What do you think about abortion without parental consent for minors?

   b. Some people think the President should be able to serve more than 2 terms. What do you think?

   c. What do you like most about TV on Tuesday nights?

5. Using the survey example in Question 1, write a survey question that falls into each of the categories below. Then rewrite the question so that it is more appropriate for the purpose of the survey.

   a. double-barreled question

   b. leading question

   c. highly detailed question

   d. potentially embarrassing question

6. Using the six principles of Backstrom and Hursh-Cesar for writing successful introductions to questionnaires (page 114 of your text), write an introduction to a questionnaire for the survey-design example in Question 1.

7. List six techniques researchers use to increase the rate of return for mail surveys.

8. A private poll is being conducted by a U.S. senator to determine voter opinion of a newly proposed public policy concerning the treatment of toxic goods in the senator's home state. Design as many filter questions as necessary to determine whether or not a respondent is familiar with the policy.

9. Researcher X is conducting a survey of teenage girls to determine how much the advertising of cosmetics on TV influences their buying behavior. Describe the problems inherent in all survey research that might present difficulties in this study.

CHAPTER 7
Field Research and Related Research Methods

Although laboratory research and surveys are two widely used methods of data collection in mass media research, these methods are not suitable for all problems. In some cases, researchers find that they must conduct research in a natural setting in the form of <u>field experiments</u>.

Chapter 7 discusses the advantages and disadvantages of field experiments, field observation, focus groups, and case studies.

<u>Field experiments</u> are carried out on the subject's "turf" as opposed to in a laboratory. Because they are not influenced by the artificiality of the laboratory, their main advantage is external validity.

<u>Field observation studies</u> are also used by researchers to study phenomenon under natural circumstances. Although it is a flexible research method, field observation presents difficulties in achieving external validity.

<u>Focus groups</u>, or <u>group interviewing</u>, are most often used to gather preliminary data, while <u>case studies</u> draw information from as many sources as possible to explain a particular phenomenon.

NAME _____

CLASS _____

DATE _____

<u>RESEARCH TERMS</u>

Use the space provided below to define the following terms.

1. Case study (155)

2. Field experiment (138)

3. Field observation (144)

4. Focus group (151)

5. Focused interview (158)

6. Individual focus sessions (155)

7. Open-ended interview (158)

8. Protocol (158)

9. Reactivity (139)

10. Total observation (145)

11. Total participation (145)

REVIEW QUESTIONS

Choose one response that best answers each question below.

1. An advantage of conducting field experiments over other research methodologies is (139)

    a. there is a greater degree of internal validity
    b. there is a greater degree of external validity
    c. demand characteristics are significant
    d. they have the characteristic of reactivity
    e. b and c are correct

2. Researchers often prefer other methodologies over field experiments because (140)

    a. of ethical considerations
    b. researchers want to be able to control all variables
    c. sampling expenses are high
    d. field experiments elicit too much detail
    e. a and b are correct

3. The primary <u>difference</u> between field experiments and laboratory research is (138)

   a. statistical control
   b. the setting
   c. absence of rules to control subject awareness
   d. external validity
   e. none of the above

4. Field experiments <u>do not</u> allow researchers to (140)

   a. manipulate independent variables
   b. take advantage of existing conditions
   c. study complex social problems
   d. control intervening variables
   e. c and d are correct

5. Using the method of <u>field observation</u> to collect data often presents the problem of (147)

   a. experimenter bias
   b. collection of insufficient data for pilot studies
   c. defining background information necessary to form a hypothesis
   d. access to subjects otherwise difficult to examine
   e. a and d are correct

6. The most significant <u>advantage</u> of field observation over laboratory and survey research is (146)

   a. increased external validity
   b. ease of quantifying data
   c. increased accuracy of data collection
   d. collection of data rich in detail
   e. c and d are correct

7. Which of the following is the <u>criticism</u> mentioned most often with respect to field observation? (147)

   a. reactivity
   b. lack of external validity
   c. prohibitive cost
   d. frequent sampling error
   e. respondent bias

8. The sampling technique used most often in field observation is (149)

   a. probability sampling
   b. random sampling
   c. purposive sampling
   d. available sampling
   e. quota sampling

9. The identifying characteristic of a focus group is (151)

   a. controlled discussion
   b. the gathering of preliminary quantitative data
   c. ease of measurement
   d. external validity
   e. a and b are correct

10. An advantage of using focus groups over other research methods is (151)

    a. questions are rigidly designed and easy to deliver
    b. they provide answers indicating "how much"
    c. they allow the collection of preliminary information for a study
    d. sample size is small and easy to obtain
    e. b and c are correct

11. Triangulation is used to (147)

    a. cross-validate results
    b. supplement observational data
    c. analyze complex data
    d. gather representative samples
    e. a and c are correct

12. Sampling in field observation differs from other research methods because (148)

    a. it's unclear who should participate
    b. it's unclear how many should be observed
    c. it's more difficult to obtain a random sample
    d. it's difficult to generalize data to a larger population
    e. none of the above

13. Individual focus group sessions <u>differ</u> from group focus sessions in that they (155)

    a. eliminate the phenomenon of group pressure
    b. can be conducted in a shorter amount of time
    c. eliminate the potential for experimenter fatigue
    d. permit the gathering of large amounts of information
    e. a and d are correct

14. The <u>case study method</u> is used when researchers want to (155)

    a. understand or explain a phenomenon
    b. collect a large amount of detailed information
    c. gather preliminary and background data
    d. conduct exploratory research
    e. a and b are correct

15. A <u>disadvantage</u> of using a case study is (159)

    a. expense
    b. generation of data that cannot be summarized
    c. the likelihood of idiosyncratic and unique results
    d. difficulty in generalizing data
    e. b and d are correct

16. Researchers are conducting a study to determine if there is a trend toward acceptance of pornography. Which <u>method</u> below would they be most likely to use? (156)

    a. focus group
    b. case study
    c. field observation
    d. individual focus group
    e. any of the above

RELATIONAL DEFINITIONS

In each example provided below, choose the one term or concept that does not fit with the others. Explain why.

1. gaining access/sampling/focus group/exiting (148)

2. design/data collection/measurement/data analysis (157)

3. ethical considerations/external hindrances/gaining permission/inexpensive (140)

4. external validity/nonreactivity/complex social topics/external hindrances (139)

5. controlled discussion/simultaneous interviewing/preliminary data/telephone study (151)

6. collecting data/generating theories/description/quantification (145)

7. external validity/experimenter bias/detailed data/lack of control (147)

CONCEPT APPLICATION QUESTIONS

1. As a researcher, you have been asked to conduct a study to determine the effectiveness of a new public relations campaign for Ford Motor Company. Decide whether your study should use the methodology of a field experiment, field observation, a focus group, or a case study. Defend your choice to your client, indicating the advantages of your choice as well as the disadvantages of the methods you did not choose.

2. Your research partner wants to study the effectiveness of announcements identifying commercials on Saturday morning children's programs on children's ability to differentiate between ads and entertainment. Your partner is convinced the study would best be approached in the controlled conditions of the laboratory. You, on the other hand, prefer to approach the problem with a field experiment. On which issues will you agree and disagree?

3. Since 1980, only 2-3% of the articles published in journalism and broadcasting journals have employed the research technique of the field observation. Recently, however, more and more researchers are considering this methodology as a viable approach. Define a mass media problem that might use field observation, and explain why you think the field observation method would be superior to others.

4. Using the example in Question 3 of a study using the field observation method, explain the five stages you will follow to conduct your study.

5. As a researcher, you have been asked by a radio station to conduct an image study that needs to be done quickly and inexpensively. You tell the client you want to conduct a focus group and then a telephone survey. Why?

6. Develop a mass media research topic that would be appropriate for a case study. Define the advantages and disadvantages of using this method.

CHAPTER 8
Content Analysis

During the past decade, content analysis has become an increasingly popular method of studying the symbols and messages contained in mass media.

Chapter 8 focuses on content analysis as a technique for evaluating aspects of messages unique to a particular medium. For example, researchers might use content analysis to investigate the use of words depicting violence on television cartoons.

Some of the purposes of content analysis include describing the content of messages at one or more points in time, comparing what is said in the media to what actually exists in the real world, and assessing media images of particular minority or ethnic groups in society.

As in laboratory, survey, and field methodologies, the use of content analysis requires close adherence to explicit rules and procedures, as well as systematic evaluation. For the most part, content analysis is conducted in several clearly defined stages.

Although this research technique provides an efficient way to study the content of media messages, it also has limitations as a research tool. For example, content analysis cannot serve as a basis for making statements about the _effects_ of content on an audience.

This chapter reviews the procedure of content analysis from problem definition to analysis of data.

NAME   _____

CLASS   _____

DATE   _____

RESEARCH TERMS

Use the space provided below to define the following terms.

1. Category system (175)

2. Coding (179)

3. Concurrent validity (186)

4. Construct validity (187)

5. Content analysis (166)

6. Cultivation analysis (169)

7. "Defining the universe" (172)

8. Descriptive studies (168)

9. Exhaustivity (177)

10. Face validity (186)

11. Intercoder reliability (177)

12. Medium variables (167)

13. Predictive validity (187)

14. Unit of analysis (174)

REVIEW QUESTIONS

Choose one response that best answers each question below.

1. Which of the following best defines the technique of content analysis? (166)

   a. a research method for analyzing data in their context
   b. studying data in a systematic and subjective manner
   c. a method for discovering "meaning" of messages
   d. a method that offers flexibility in evaluating messages
   e. a method of studying messages for the purpose of measuring variables

2. A definition of content analysis in mass media research is (166)

   a. a method to measure ideas in a systematic way
   b. a technique for interpreting the meaning of communication in a particular context
   c. a way of analyzing communication in an objective manner
   d. a method of systematically quantifying communication usage for the purpose of measuring variables
   e. a systematic and subjective methodology for studying communication content

3. Which of the following procedures is required in content analysis? (166)

   a. subjectivity
   b. systematic selection and evaluation
   c. census
   d. multistage sampling
   e. b and d are correct

4. Systematic evaluation in content analysis means (166)

   a. sampling selection must follow proper procedures
   b. every item must have an equal chance of being included in the analysis
   c. operational definitions should be explicit
   d. coders must all be exposed to the material for the same length of time
   e. only one set of guidelines for evaluation is used in a study

5. <u>Objectivity</u> in content analysis means (166)

   a. a clear set of criteria and procedures must be established
   b. rules for classification of variables should be the same for all studies
   c. the unit of analysis should be selected randomly
   d. there must be no opportunity for experimenter bias
   e. a and d are correct

6. The <u>goal</u> of content analysis is to (166)

   a. measure repetition of ideas
   b. quantify phenomena
   c. accurately represent a body of messages
   d. categorize independent variables
   e. measure symbols and messages and compare them over time

7. Which of the following is <u>not</u> a purpose of content analysis? (167)

   a. testing hypotheses of form
   b. assessing minority images
   c. studying complex social situations
   d. serving as a starting point for subsequent studies
   e. none of the above

8. Which of the following is <u>not</u> a limitation of content analysis? (170)

   a. results limited to definitions used in a particular study
   b. a lack of messages relevant to research
   c. the ability to define effects of contents on audiences
   d. expense
   e. the ability to document social trends

9. A <u>medium variable</u> is used in content analysis to (167)

   a. offset interference of confounding variables
   b. categorize aspects of content unique to the medium being studied
   c. ensure the characteristic of equivalence in a study
   d. generalize a unit of analysis to similar studies
   e. a and b are correct

10. <u>Cultivation analysis</u> is used to (169)

    a. uncover "hidden" categories for analysis
    b. document the effects of dominant messages and themes on attitudes
    c. analyze attitudes described in a particular medium
    d. study the influence of media messages on real-life situations
    e. b and d are correct

11. The most common type of <u>sample selection</u> in content analysis involves (172)

    a. conducting a census
    b. multistage sampling
    c. a simple random sample
    d. constructing a composite week
    e. determining the incidence of the phenomenon in question

12. A <u>strength</u> of the content analysis methodology in studying mass media is that (167)

    a. researchers can discover why certain messages affect audiences positively or negatively
    b. it can be used as a starting point for subsequent studies
    c. definitions and categories of one study can be used to measure similar concepts in other studies
    d. it is an inexpensive and easily applicable methodology for studying the effects of messages in communication
    e. messages relevant to research are readily available

13. The <u>first step</u> a researcher must take to conduct a content analysis is to (171)

    a. articulate a hypothesis
    b. formulate constitutive definitions of the population to be studied
    c. define what will be measured and identify content categories
    d. define the universe
    e. c and d are correct

14. A common problem in sampling with content analysis is (174)

    a. the possibility of using too few source dates, which results in an unrepresentative sample
    b. random selection runs the risk of a study being atypical
    c. the difficulty of determining an adequate sampling
    d. the possibility of systematic bias in the content itself
    e. a and d are correct

15. A unit of analysis in content analysis (174)

    a. must share criteria for inclusion in a study
    b. is that which is counted in a study
    c. is the largest unit of analysis
    d. is a definition of a communicative act
    e. a and b are correct

16. The characteristic of exhaustivity in content analysis categories (177)

    a. occurs when a unit of analysis does not fit in a predetermined category
    b. occurs when a unit of analysis can be placed in one and only one category
    c. is solved with categories labeled "other"
    d. exists when there is a category for every unit of analysis
    e. c and d are correct

17. Exclusivity in content analysis refers to when units of analysis (177)

    a. are placed in more than one category
    b. fall simultaneously into two or more categories
    c. are exhaustive and reliable
    d. can be placed in only one category
    e. c and d are correct

18. Intercoder reliability in content analysis (177)

    a. is an unquantifiable characteristic of content analysis
    b. is rarely eliminated even with pretesting of category systems
    c. decreases when a study has too many categories
    d. can be achieved by combining several categories
    e. refers to agreement among coders about categories used

19. Which of the following levels of data measurement is generally not used in content analysis? (178)

    a. multivariate
    b. ratio
    c. ordinal
    d. interval
    e. nominal

20. When quantifying content analysis at the nominal level, researchers (178)

    a. are concerned with developing subjective categories of attributes
    b. count how often a unit occurs in each category
    c. often find a lowering of intercoder reliability
    d. discover the optimum number of content categories
    e. c and d are correct

21. Placing a unit of analysis into a content category is called (179)

    a. establishing a quantifying system
    b. content sampling
    c. ratio level measurement
    d. coding
    e. b and d are correct

22. One way to determine intercoder reliability is to (183)

    a. reanalyze a subsample of the data
    b. take into account agreement by chance
    c. calculate the percentage of agreement
    d. lower the amount of judgmental leeway given to coders
    e. have coders code the same data twice

23. A content analysis is said to be <u>reliable</u> when (182)

   a. similar studies result in similar conclusions
   b. categories are defined with maximum detail
   c. less than 5% of coders disagree about definition categories
   d. independent coders place units of analysis in similar categories
   e. a repeated measure of the same content results in similar decisions

24. <u>Validity</u> in content analysis is <u>not</u> influenced by (186)

   a. adequacy of definitions used
   b. low reliability
   c. overlapping categories
   d. faulty sample design
   e. the validity of the original hypothesis

25. <u>Face validity</u> in a study assumes an instrument measures what it purports to measure if (186)

   a. coders are in agreement about units of analysis and categories used
   b. analytical procedures have been adequately conducted
   c. a rigid and satisfactorily defined category system exists
   d. the results of a subsample concur with the results of the entire study
   e. b and c are correct

26. Which method is most commonly used in content analysis to <u>assess validity</u>? (187)

   a. concurrent validity
   b. predictive validity
   c. face validity
   d. constructive validity
   e. none of the above

RELATIONAL DEFINITIONS

For each example provided below, choose the <u>one</u> term or concept that does not fit with the others. Explain why.

1. systematic/qualitative/objective/interpretive (166)

2. exhaustive/mutually exclusive/reliable/specific (177)

3. coder/category definitions/unit of analysis/validity/coding instructions (182)

4. societal change/controversial issues/personality tests/radio listenership (168)

5. face/concurrent/predictive/reliable (186)

6. popular songs/Library of Congress/propaganda/historical documents (165)

CONCEPT APPLICATION QUESTIONS

1. Content analysis is generally used for one of five purposes. Give an example of a mass media research project that would illustrate each of these purposes.

2. As a researcher, you want to design a content analysis study to show how slang phrases in one adolescent generation reappear decades later in another adolescent generation but with different interpretations. Define the specific steps you will follow in conducting this study. Why is each step necessary?

3. Provide an operational definition for the unit of analysis that could be used by the researchers in the study described in Question 2.

4. Define the characteristics of <u>category systems</u> used in content analysis. What categories might the researchers use in the study described in Question 2?

5. Using the example in Question 2, explain how the researchers might use the multistage sampling technique to select a sample for their study.

6. What types of information will the researchers need to share with those who will be coding the study in Question 2?

7. In interpreting the results of the study described in Question 2, what does it mean that the researchers may be faced with the "fully/only" dilemma?

8. Once completed, the study in Question 2 is found to be unreliable. Where can the researchers look to determine why the results have failed to achieve reliability?

9. Describe a mass media study wherein a researcher could use the technique of cultivation analysis. What are some of the drawbacks of this type of study?

10. There are difficulties in sampling peculiar to the method of content analysis. Using the example of the study defined in Question 2, explain how you would account for and eliminate these types of sampling difficulties?

11. You are conducting a content analysis of how children are portrayed in commercials promoting adult products. Develop a scale for coders who will be watching the commercials and rating the units of analysis.

12. In the study example in Question 11, Coder A and Coder B agree on 55 coding decisions out of a possible 75. What is the reliability in terms of percentage of agreement? What is a drawback of this method of determining intercoder reliability?

13. Suppose that two coders are assigning topics of conversation between people on their first date into five categories and obtain the following distribution. Assume the coders agree on 85% of their classifications. Calculate Scott's pi index (page 184 of your text). Explain how this method of determining percentage of intercoder reliability is different from that computed in Question 12.

Category	Percent of Agreement
1. family	35%
2. career goals	25%
3. personal background	20%
4. hobbies/interests	15%
5. school activities	5%

CHAPTER 9
Longitudinal Research

Longitudinal research involves the collection of data at different points in time. Although this methodology has been used for decades in the behavioral sciences, its use in mass media research has been infrequent. However, several longitudinal mass media studies <u>have</u> contributed significantly to the evolution of mass media research by measuring both subtle and cumulative mass media effects.

The three types of longitudinal studies used in mass media research include: <u>the trend study</u>, <u>the cohort analysis</u>, and <u>the panel study</u>.

<u>Trend studies</u> ask the same questions of different groups of people at different points in time.

<u>Cohort studies</u> measure (at two or more points in time) a characteristic of a sample whose members share some significant life event (for example, time of birth).

<u>Panel studies</u> measure the same sample of respondents at different points in time. Unlike trend studies and cohort studies, panel studies allow researchers to make statements about the casual ordering of the variables being studied.

NAME _____

CLASS _____

DATE _____

RESEARCH TERMS

Using the space provided below define the following terms.

1. Age effects (198)

2. Catch-up panel (204)

3. Cohort (196)

4. Cohort analysis (195)

5. Cohort effect (197)

6. Continuous panel (201)

7. Cross-sectional research (194)

8. Follow-back panel (204)

9. Intercohort differences (198)

10. Interval panel (201)

11. Longitudinal research (194)

12. Panel study (200)

13. Period effect (198)

14. Retrospective panel (203)

15. Trend study (195)

REVIEW QUESTIONS

Choose <u>one</u> response that <u>best</u> answers each question below.

1. The most common type of <u>longitudinal study</u> in mass media research is (195)

    a. cohort analysis
    b. cross-sectional
    c. trend study
    d. retrospective panel
    e. panel study

2. The process of collecting data from a representative sample <u>at one point in time</u> is called (194)

    a. cross-lagged correlation
    b. longitudinal research
    c. cohort analysis
    d. a trend study
    e. cross-sectional research

3. A <u>trend study</u> samples (195)

    a. data collected from a representative sample at one point in time
    b. specific populations as they change over time
    c. different groups of people from the same population at different times
    d. people who share a significant life event
    e. attitudes about various facets of social behavior

4. <u>Trend studies</u> provide information about (195)

    a. gross and net changes
    b. long-term changes in a population
    c. specific attitudes or behavior patterns
    d. net changes
    e. b and d are correct

5. In a study of pre-election voting behavior of rural women in the last statewide election, a <u>trend study</u> would show (195)

   a. percentage of votes cast per candidate
   b. changes in party affiliation
   c. percentage of voters who changed their mind about a candidate before the final ballot
   d. number of voters who never changed their minds
   e. c and d are correct

6. An <u>advantage</u> of a trend study is (196)

   a. it is valuable in describing both short- and long-term changes in populations
   b. it can rely on secondary analysis of survey data
   c. it provides data describing media and audience conduct
   d. it allows researchers to make statements about effects of variables
   e. there is little problem with sample mortality

7. A <u>cohort</u> is defined as (196)

   a. groups who share perceptions
   b. populations who experience similar life events at the same time
   c. individuals who share a significant life event within a given period of time
   d. a sample of the population who share a common characteristic
   e. c and d are correct

8. Which of the following is <u>not</u> an example of a cohort? (196)

   a. everyone with birthdays in August in modern times
   b. everyone who died between the years 1927-1947
   c. college graduates in the Class of 1983
   d. persons who evaded the draft and went to Canada in 1968
   e. students who dropped out of college and joined the war effort in Vietnam

9. A <u>cohort analysis</u> attempts to measure (197)

   a. changes in a dependent variable
   b. how certain individuals within a cohort change over time
   c. characteristics of one cohort at two or more points in time
   d. characteristics of one or more cohorts at two or more points in time
   e. a and d are correct

10. For cohorts to be measured <u>over time</u>, the following must be equal (197)

    a. intervals between periods of measurement
    b. how a particular cohort changes over time
    c. sex
    d. number of cohorts in each group
    e. all of the above

11. Among other things, <u>cohort analyses</u> tell us (198)

    a. how individuals in a cohort change over time
    b. why cohorts change over time
    c. age effects
    d. period effects
    e. c and d are correct

12. A <u>pure period effect</u> (199)

    a. reveals variation by age at any period
    b. depicts identical variations from one period of time to another
    c. shows changes in cohorts equal to the average change in population
    d. reveals that the dependent variable is affected by maturation
    e. b and c are correct

13. Which of the following is <u>not</u> a cohort effect? (198)

    a. maturation
    b. time period
    c. sex
    d. age
    e. values

14. Researchers who use cohort analysis are at a <u>disadvantage</u> because (199)

    a. they can only detect net changes
    b. of the likelihood of sample mortality
    c. public opinion is difficult to measure
    d. effects of age, cohort, and period are often confounded
    e. b and d are correct

15. <u>Panel studies</u> are useful in (200)

    a. discovering how a group of individuals change over time
    b. predicting cause-and-effect relationships
    c. revealing information about gross changes in the dependent variable
    d. indicating possible future changes in group behavior
    e. a and b are correct

16. Which of the following is <u>not</u> a disadvantage of panel studies? (201)

    a. interviewer bias
    b. subject sensitization
    c. mortality
    d. expense
    e. respondent error

17. A <u>retrospective panel</u> is advantageous because (203)

    a. it does not require two waves of data for analysis
    b. it is easier to measure what has already occurred
    c. a smaller sample size is required
    d. changes over many years can be analyzed in a short time
    e. a and d are correct

18. Which is <u>not</u> a disadvantage of a catch-up panel? (204)

    a. many variables necessary to the study no longer exist
    b. the availability of baseline archival data
    c. incompatibility of measures, past and present
    d. new variables cannot be considered
    e. none of the above

19. Which of the following panel studies uses <u>archival data</u> to create the <u>longitudinal dimensions</u> of a study? (204)

    a. retrospective
    b. catch-up
    c. follow-back
    d. continuous
    e. interval

20. Which of the following methodologies allows researchers to predict about <u>causal relationships</u> among variables? (205)

    a. cross-lagged correlation
    b. trend study
    c. cross-sectional survey
    d. panel study
    e. cohort study

RELATIONAL DEFINITIONS

In each example below, choose the **one** term or concept that does not fit with the others. Explain why.

1. trend study/panel study/cross-sectional research/cohort analysis (194)

2. different groups/same time/same population/different times (195)

3. secondary analysis/gross changes/long-term changes/net changes (196)

4. given period of time/shared life experience/group of individuals/ cohort effect (197)

5. points in time/multiple cohorts/single cohort/shared characteristics (197)

6. age/cohort/period/sampling (198)

7. same sample/same time/different points in time/net and gross changes (200)

8. mortality/sample refusals/sensitization/inexpensive (202)

9. retrospective/interval/follow-back/catch-up (203)

CONCEPT APPLICATION QUESTIONS

1. Longitudinal studies, as opposed to cross-sectional research, have been used infrequently in mass media research. What characteristics of mass media would make this a less likely methodology for researchers to use?

2. Identify two types of audience behavior for which a trend study could be conducted. Identify possible subjects, variables, and a research design to provide information about net changes in these behaviors.

3. Referring to the table below, identify the following:

   a. cohort

   b. the dependent variable(s)

   c. cohort effect(s)

Percentage Who Regularly Attend Horror Movies

Age	1984	1985	1986
10-20	9	10	12
21-30	10	11	12
31-40	6	7	6

4. Discuss the major difference between a cross-sectional survey and a panel study with regard to analyzing causation.

5. For each of the types of panel designs listed below, design a mass media research question for which the methodology would be applicable, and explain why the panel design you have chosen is superior to the others.

   a. retrospective

   b. follow-back

   c. catch-up

6. Define a specific cohort and a cohort effect characteristic. With these data, identify how differences in this characteristic might be explained by cohort analysis.

PART THREE
Basic Statistics

10 INTRODUCTION TO STATISTICS

11 HYPOTHESIS TESTING

12 INFERENTIAL STATISTICS

CHAPTER 10
Introduction to Statistics

Statistics provide mathematical models for organizing, summarizing, and analyzing data collected and measured with the research methodologies described in previous chapters.

Chapter 10 introduces the two types of statistical procedures used by mass media researchers: <u>descriptive</u> and <u>inferential</u>.

In learning any statistical procedure, it is crucial to realize that although statistics can produce valid results, they do so only if the data variables they comprise have been established scientifically. Thus, a research study that is poorly conceived and/or conducted cannot be salvaged by a statistical technique.

NAME _____

CLASS _____

DATE _____

RESEARCH TERMS

Use the space provided below to define the following terms.

1. Coefficient of determination (233)

2. Coefficient of nondetermination (233)

3. Central tendency (218)

4. Descriptive statistics (213)

5. Deviation scores (222)

6. Dispersion (221)

7. Distribution (213)

8. Frequency curve (216)

9. Frequency distribution (214)

10. Frequency polygon (215)

11. Graph (215)

12. Histogram (215)

13. Inferential statistics (237)

14. Kurtosis (217)

15. Leptokurtic distribution (217)

16. Mean (219)

17. Median (219)

18. Mesokurtic distribution (217)

19. Mode (218)

20. Normal curve (217)

21. Platykurtic distribution (217)

22. Population distribution (238)

23. Range (221)

24. Sample distribution (237)

25. Sampling distribution (238)

26. Scattergram (229)

27. Simple linear regression (234)

28. Skewness (217)

29. Standard deviation (224)

30. Standard scores (224)

31. Summary statistics (218)

32. Variance (222)

33. x-axis (215)

34. y-axis (215)

REVIEW QUESTIONS

Choose one response that best answers each question below.

1. Descriptive statistics as opposed to inferential statistics (213)

    a. collect numbers
    b. distribute meaningful data in tables
    c. determine how much data can be generalized to larger populations
    d. indicate the conclusions researchers can draw from data collected
    e. organize and summarize data for interpretation

2. The most basic type of statistically organized data is (213)

    a. two data columns
    b. a frequency distribution
    c. a distribution
    d. grouped intervals
    e. lists of variables and occurrences

3. Among other things, frequency distributions cannot display (214)

    a. individual scores
    b. frequency of occurrence
    c. cumulative frequency
    d. percentage of response
    e. mathematical patterns

4. The y-axis of a graph typically displays (215)

    a. scores
    b. order by magnitude
    c. relative frequency of data
    d. cumulative frequency
    e. percentage of response

163

5. A <u>frequency polygon</u> differs from a <u>frequency curve</u> in that a frequency polygon (216)

   a. measures midpoints of intervals
   b. connects intervals only on the <u>x</u>-axis
   c. curves rather than connects dots
   d. indicates irregularities due to chance
   e. a and d are correct

6. Researchers who use a <u>frequency curve</u> to plot data assume (217)

   a. a random sampling was used
   b. the variable was distributed continuously over the population
   c. a frequency polygon would fail to indicate the role of chance
   d. a normal curve is necessary
   e. b and c are correct

7. Which of the following is <u>not</u> described as a deviation from a normal curve? (217)

   a. many scores centered around the center of a distribution
   b. scores spread over a wide area of the y-axis
   c. collection of scores around a point on the y-axis
   d. half the data on one side of the midpoint, half on the other
   e. data collected at one end of an axis

8. A <u>platykurtic distribution</u> deviates from a normal curve because (217)

   a. the tail of the curve peaks off to the right
   b. the halves of the curve are equal
   c. scores are widely dispersed
   d. scores concentrate in two areas
   e. b and c are correct

9. Plotted data that are skewed or have the characteristic of
   kurtosis (217)

   a. must be manipulated to achieve more normal distribution
   b. deviates so far from the norm that the data are not valid
   c. shows no relation to a normal curve, and therefore
      is not representative of all populations
   d. reveals that errors have been made in data collection
   e. c and d are correct

10. Once data have been distributed, they (218)

    a. require preliminary interpretation
    b. must be further organized
    c. must be manipulated or transformed
    d. must be condensed to measure distribution tendencies
    e. must be summarized

11. Central tendency as opposed to dispersion (221)

    a. shows deviation from the mean
    b. refers to the midpoint of distribution
    c. determines a typical score of a distribution
    d. calculates a typical score
    e. includes the mode and mean

12. The central tendency measurement that has the most drawbacks
    as a descriptive statistic is (218)

    a. the median
    b. the mode
    c. the mean
    d. $\underline{N}$
    e. dispersion

13. A mean is defined as (219)

    a. accounting for only extreme scores
    b. the sum of all scores, divided by $\underline{N}$
    c. the sum of the midpoints of intervals
    d. the average of a set of scores
    e. b and d are correct

14. If data are calculated at the <u>nominal level</u>, which of the following is/are meaningful? (221)

    a. mean
    b. median
    c. mode
    d. mean and mode
    e. mean and median

15. If data are calculated at the <u>ordinal level</u>, which of the following is/are meaningful? (221)

    a. mean
    b. mode
    c. median
    d. mean and mode
    e. mode and median

16. Before researchers can decide which measures of <u>central tendency</u> to report for a set of data, they must consider (221)

    a. whether the goal is to describe data
    b. if the purpose is only to summarize data
    c. the level of measurement
    d. the purpose of the statistic
    e. c and d are correct

17. Statistics that measure <u>dispersion</u> (221)

    a. reflect differences between distributions
    b. reflect data related to a central point
    c. describe how data collect at particular scores in a distribution
    d. are concerned with data between extreme points
    e. a and c are correct

18. Which of the following is <u>not</u> a measure of dispersion? (221)

    a. central tendency
    b. range
    c. standard deviation
    d. variance
    e. the difference between high and low scores

19. The measure of variance (222)

    a. indicates scores that are widely scattered
    b. provides an index of deviation from the median
    c. represents the dispersion of data within a range
    d. indicates the degree to which scores deviate from the mean
    e. is the sum of the square of deviation scores

20. A drawback of the measure of variance is that (223)

    a. it is expressed as a square root
    b. it requires an additional statistical step of calculating standard deviation
    c. it is not expressed in terms of the original measurement
    d. it reveals only the distance of the scores from the mean
    e. b and c are correct

21. Standard scores for any distribution of data are derived by (226)

    a. comparisons between dissimilar instruments
    b. determining the median and standard deviation
    c. indicating the placement of a score in relation to the mean
    d. revealing the frequency of occurrence of variables
    e. a and d are correct

22. Standard scores used in conjunction with the normal curve (226)

    a. possess the properties of a z-score distribution
    b. allow statements to be made regarding how often certain variables occur
    c. allow researchers to make important predictive statements
    d. are equal to standard deviation divided by 2
    e. are rarely used in mass media research

23. When the degree to which two variables change in relation to each other is expressed numerically, this is called (229)

    a. positive relationship
    b. measures of association
    c. inverse relationship
    d. correlation
    e. b and d are correct

24. Scattergrams are used to (229)

    a. measure inverse relationships between two or more variables
    b. portray any relationship between two or more variables
    c. make two different measurements of the same variable
    d. portray positive, then negative, relationships between two variables
    e. show how one variable increases while the other decreases

25. A relationship between two variables is said to be curvilinear when (229)

    a. both variables increase incrementally
    b. high scores on one variable are associated with high or low scores on another variable
    c. the relationship of two variables is positive to a point, then becomes inverse
    d. the relationship of two variables is inverse to a point, then becomes positive
    e. c and d are correct

26. One song included on the "Hot Buttered Soul" album by Issac Hayes is

    a. "Heard It Through the Grapevine"
    b. "Papa's Got a Brand New Bag"
    c. "Hyperbolicsyllabicsesquedalymistic"
    d. "Shaft's Big Score"
    e. "FTD (The Handyman)"

RELATIONAL DEFINITIONS

In each example provided below, choose the one term or concept that does not fit with the others. Explain why.

1. organizing/summarizing/measuring/analyzing (213)

2. data reduction/inferential/data distribution/summary statistics (213)

3. tables/histogram/graphs/generalized results (213)

4. variance/frequency of occurrence/magnitude/possible score (214)

5. mesokurtic/skewness/normal curve/kurtosis (217)

6. description/central tendency/variability/dispersion (218)

7. mode/range/median/mean (218)

8. range/variance/standard deviation/standard scores (221)

9. high score/dispersion/mean/low score (221)

10. $\underline{X}$ variable/numerical expression/measure of association/correlation (229)

11. method of prediction/degrees of change/variables/sample distribution (234)

CONTENT APPLICATION QUESTIONS

1. Referring to the frequency distribution table below, determine the following:

   a. N

   b. response percentage

   c. cumulative frequency (cf)

   d. cf percentage of N

Hours	Frequency
0.1	5
0.2	4
1.0	3
2.5	5
1.0	1
4.0	2

2. Referring to the table in Question 1, determine the following characteristics of central tendency. Which of these three measures would a researcher most likely report for this set of data if the data represented nominal measurements?

   a. mode

   b. median

   c. mean

3. Using the data you compiled from Questions 1 and 2, determine the following measures of variation or dispersion:

   a. range

   b. variance

   c. deviation scores

   d. standard deviation

   e. standard scores

4. Referring to Table 10.6 on page 227 of your text, suppose that newspaper reading by adults is normally distributed with a mean of 1 hour per day and a standard deviation of 0.3 hour. What proportion of the population reads between 1.3 and 1.6 hours per day?

5. A researcher conducts a study to determine the relationship between the number of hours students study and their performance on an objective exam. Refer to the scattergrams on page 231 of your text. Which one would most likely display the probable results of this research study? Explain.

6. Explain why the notion of probability is important in inferential statistics.

CHAPTER 11
Hypothesis Testing

In beginning a research test, all researchers must start with some tentative generalizations regarding a relationship between two or more variables. Thus, the initial step for a researcher is to develop a statement or a question to test.

Chapter 11 describes two methods mass media researchers use to develop <u>research questions</u> and <u>statistical hypotheses</u>. The two are identical except for the aspect of prediction: hypotheses predict an experimental outcome, research questions do not.

NAME _____

CLASS _____

DATE _____

RESEARCH TERMS

Use the space provided below to define the following terms.

1. Effects size (255)

2. Exploratory research (246)

3. Hypothesis (247)

4. Null hypothesis (249)

5. One-tail test (250)

6. Power (255)

7. Probability level (250)

8. Region of rejection (250)

9. Research question (246)

10. Significance testing (255)

11. Two-tail test (251)

12. Type I error (253)

13. Type II error (253)

RESEARCH QUESTIONS

Choose **one** response that **best** answers each question below.

1. The primary difference between a <u>research question</u> and a <u>hypothesis</u> is (246)

    a. research questions cannot be tested for statistical significance
    b. hypotheses are developed to determine causality
    c. hypotheses predict an experimental outcome
    d. research questions are not based on theory
    e. none of the above

2. Which of the following is not considered a benefit of a hypothesis for researchers? (247)

   a. it allows for quantification of variables
   b. it rules out intervening variables
   c. it provides an indication of the sequence of steps to follow
   d. it eliminates error in research
   e. it eliminates trial-and-error research

3. Which of the following does not characterize a useful hypothesis? (248)

   a. a background of supporting evidence
   b. logical consistency
   c. testability
   d. random relationships
   e. parsimonious form

4. The null hypothesis is important to researchers because (249)

   a. it asserts that statistical differences are not due to chance or random error
   b. it must be accepted or rejected before the study can be conducted
   c. it is an alternative hypothesis for testing
   d. it is used to determine the statistical significance of a research study
   e. b and d are correct

5. Probability levels are used to (250)

   a. determine the probability of committing a Type I error
   b. determine the region of rejection
   c. determine the level of significance
   d. accept or reject the research hypothesis
   e. a and d are correct

6. Establishing a level of significance depends on (250)

   a. the purpose of the study
   b. the level of probability
   c. the amount of acceptable error
   d. the region of rejection
   e. a and c are correct

7. The <u>region of rejection</u> is (250)

    a. the level of significance chosen by the researcher
    b. located in the center of the sampling distribution
    c. used to define the dimension of a sampling distribution
    d. the proportion of the area in which the null hypothesis is rejected
    e. c and d are correct

8. The term <u>one-tail test</u> refers to (250)

    a. a type of prediction
    b. a test used when little information about a research area is available
    c. results that are predicted or calculated as positive or negative
    d. positive results only
    e. a and c are correct

9. <u>Type I error</u> in hypothesis testing refers to (253)

    a. acceptance of a null hypothesis that should be rejected
    b. rejection of a null hypothesis that should be accepted
    c. error that is not under the control of the researcher
    d. error that is under the control of the researcher
    e. b and d are correct

10. <u>Type II error</u> in hypothesis testing (253)

    a. does not depend on the significant effect of a study
    b. is dependent on the probability level
    c. refers to data that are conversely proportional to the level of Type I error
    d. refers to error controlled by the design of the experiment
    e. b and d are correct

11. In reference to the results of a study, significance testing (255)

    a. concludes that studies that find significant results are of greater value
    b. helps researchers rule out worthless variables
    c. indicates that it is of value to propose a null hypothesis as a research hypothesis
    d. determines the error variance in a study
    e. b and c are correct

12. The concept of power in a research hypothesis (255)

    a. refers to the likelihood of rejecting a null hypothesis when an alternative is true
    b. is unrelated to variance of error
    c. confirms that a phenomenon under study actually exists
    d. is a function of sample size and independent variables
    e. a and c are correct

13. Effects size, unlike probability level, (255)

    a. is not a function of statistical power
    b. is the degree to which the null hypothesis is rejected
    c. cannot be stated in exact terms
    d. is inversely proportional to the degree to which the phenomenon under study is present
    e. b and d are correct

14. A determination of power is important because (256)

    a. if a high power level allows researchers to attain a statistical significance, a Type I error may result
    b. a low power level may help in interpretation of results
    c. a low power level may result in Type II error
    d. researchers rarely know the exact level of effects size
    e. it validates the results of a study

RELATIONAL DEFINITIONS

In each example provided below, choose the <u>one</u> term or concept that does not fit with the others. Explain why.

1. research question/prediction/general indications/statistical significance (246)

2. current/parsimonious/inconsistent/testable (248)

3. research hypothesis/hypothesis of no difference/alternative hypothesis/statistical difference (249)

4. region of rejection/statistical significance/null hypothesis/significance level (250)

5. one-tail test/region of rejection/Type I error/two-tail test (250)

6. research hypothesis/null hypothesis/Type I error/Type II error (253)

7. sample size/probability level/effects size/Type I error (255)

CONCEPT APPLICATION QUESTIONS

1. Why would a researcher choose to use a research question over a hypothesis?

2. Why should hypotheses or research questions be used in the first place? Why should researchers not simply approach a problem with no preconceived ideas?

3. If a researcher does not find statistically significant results to accept or reject a hypothesis, does this make the study a waste of time? Explain.

4. Why should a researcher consider previous research when formulating a research question or hypothesis? Refer to information presented in earlier chapters to answer the question.

5. Is there ever a way in which a researcher could eliminate the need for a research question or hypothesis? Explain.

CHAPTER 12
Inferential Statistics

Because mass media researchers often want to do more than merely describe a sample, they apply inferential statistical methods to data so that they can make inferences about the population from which the sample was taken.

Chapter 12 describes some of the basic <u>inferential statistical methods</u> used in mass media research and indicates ways in which these methods may help answer research questions.

The emphasis of the chapter is on <u>using</u> statistical methods rather than on the statistical methods themselves. Although the basic formula for each statistical method discussed is given, the focus of the chapter is on how to determine the appropriateness of using a statistical method for a particular research study.

NAME _____

CLASS _____

DATE _____

RESEARCH TERMS

Use the space provided below to define the following terms.

1. Analysis of variance (270)

2. Beta weight (276)

3. Chi-square statistic (262)

4. Contingency table analysis (264)

5. Cross-tabulation (264)

6. Degrees of freedom (263)

7. Error variance (271)

8. Expected frequencies (261)

9. F ratio (271)

10. Goodness of fit (261)

11. Interaction (274)

12. Main effect (274)

13. Multiple regression (275)

14. Nonparametric statistics (260)

15. Observed frequencies (261)

16. Parametric statistics (260)

17. Partial correlation (278)

18. Principle of least squares (276)

19. Systematic variance (271)

20. t-test (267)

21. Two-way ANOVA (273)

22. Weighted linear combinations (275)

REVIEW QUESTIONS

Choose one response that best answers each question below.

1. A difference between parametric and nonparametric statistics is (261)

   a. nonparametric statistics are appropriate for interval and ratio data
   b. parametric statistics are appropriate for nominal data
   c. nonparametric statistics are used to draw inferences
   d. parametric statistics make assumptions about population parameters
   e. c and d are correct

2. Researchers use chi-square statistics to (262)

   a. show the relationship between an expected frequency and an observed frequency
   b. show the value of expected frequencies
   c. perform the goodness of fit test
   d. determine the probability level
   e. a and c are correct

3. Chi-square goodness of fit tests are used to (263)

   a. determine whether differences in frequency are significant
   b. measure variables at the interval level
   c. measure the probability of Type II error
   d. determine nonsignificant results
   e. a and d are correct

4. Before a researcher can determine goodness of fit, which of the following must be known? (263)

   a. probability level
   b. sample size
   c. degrees of freedom
   d. crosstabs
   e. a and c are correct

5. Which of the following is not a limitation of the goodness of fit test? (264)

   a. categories must be mutually exclusive
   b. each observation in a category must be independent from all others
   c. Type II error may occur
   d. variables must be measured at the interval or ratio level
   e. categories must contain at least 5 observations

6. <u>Degrees of freedom</u> refers to (263)

   a. number of scores with unknown values
   b. number of variables assigned any value
   c. number of scores free to vary in value
   d. number of categories in a goodness of fit test
   e. probability level of a study

7. The difference between the <u>goodness of fit test</u> and <u>cross-tabulation</u> is (264)

   a. researchers use cross-tabulation to determine expected frequencies
   b. only one variable can be tested in a goodness of fit test
   c. two or more variables can be tested simultaneously in a crosstab
   d. data can be summarized by a variety of measures of association in a goodness of fit test
   e. c and d are correct

8. A <u>t-test</u> in research studies (267)

   a. compares the median scores of related groups
   b. compares the mean scores of two groups
   c. assumes variables in populations are not normally distributed
   d. does not assume populations have homogeneity of variance
   e. b and d are correct

9. The <u>analysis of variance test</u> allows researchers to (270)

   a. explain systematic variance and error
   b. measure the effects of levels of dependent variables
   c. analyze factorial designs
   d. identify error
   e. a and c are correct

10. <u>Error variance</u> in data is created by (271)

    a. unknown factors
    b. unexamined or uncontrolled variables
    c. known factors that decrease all scores they influence
    d. abnormal distribution of sample data
    e. a and b are correct

11. Which of the following is <u>not</u> an assumption of the <u>ANOVA</u> method? (271)

    a. normal distribution of a sample
    b. equality in variance of groups
    c. random selection
    d. statistically dependent scores
    e. lack of concomitant relationship of variables

12. An advantage of using a <u>two-way ANOVA</u> is (274)

    a. the ability to conduct simultaneous studies for independent variables
    b. the ability to calculate effects of three or more independent variables on the dependent variable
    c. savings of time and resources
    d. interval data can be analyzed
    e. a and c are correct

13. Researchers predict the <u>dependent variable</u> by using the method of (275)

    a. multiple regression
    b. two-way ANOVA
    c. linear regression
    d. analysis of variance
    e. ANOVA

14. The primary goal of <u>multiple regression</u> is to (275)

    a. analyze the relationship between two or more independent variables and dependent variables
    b. determine the effects of many independent variables on a single dependent variable
    c. predict the dependent variable
    d. develop a formula to account for variance in the dependent variable
    e. a and d are correct

15. <u>Multiple regression</u> uses which of the following to predict the dependent variable? (276)

    a. linear combination
    b. weighting of independent variables
    c. beta weight
    d. regression coefficients
    e. none of the above

16. The basic <u>computational procedure</u> in multiple regression is known as (276)

    a. true line
    b. coefficient of correlation
    c. partial correlation
    d. the principle of least squares
    e. product moment correlation

17. Researchers use which of the following methods to determine effects of a confounding variable between an independent and dependent variable? (278)

    a. coefficient of correlation
    b. partial correlation
    c. controlling the spurious variable
    d. interaction analysis
    e. b and c are correct

RELATIONAL DEFINITIONS

In each example below, choose the <u>one</u> term or concept that does not fit with the others. Explain why.

1. nonparametric statistics/population parameters/assumptions/variance (261)

2. parametric statistics/nominal data/ordinal data/nonparametric statistics (261)

3. crosstabs/expected frequencies/chi-square/observed frequencies (262)

4. probability level/chi-square table/degrees of freedom/parametric procedures (263)

5. cross-tabulation/goodness of fit/simultaneous testing/nonparametric statistical test (264)

6. parametric statistics/median scores/two groups/statistical significance (267)

7. factorial designs/<u>t</u>-test/degrees of an independent variable/one-way (270)

8. systematic variance/systematic sampling/error variance/known and unknown factors (271)

9. simultaneous studies/independent variables/interaction/ one-way ANOVA (274)

10. prediction/analysis of independent variables/single dependent variable/analysis of variance (275)

11. independent variables/weighted/linear combination/ partial correlation (276)

12. spurious variable/influence of controlled variable/ independent variable/coefficient of correlation (279)

CONCEPT APPLICATION QUESTIONS

1. Last year a company specializing in the construction of townhomes built and sold 500 homes. The following table shows the percentage of sales for each model. Before the year started, the company expected the sales distribution percentage of all four models to be as follows: Model A, 15%; Model B, 30%; Model C, 50%; and Model D, 5%. Using these data, calculate the chi-square to determine if the company's predictions were significantly different from actual sales.

Townhome	Percent of Sales
Model A	20
Model B	40
Model C	25
Model D	15

2. Describe a mass media study where a researcher could use a
   t-test. Change the study to one where the researcher could
   use an analysis of variance.

PART FOUR
Research Applications

13 RESEARCH IN THE PRINT MEDIA

14 RESEARCH IN THE ELECTRONIC MEDIA

15 RESEARCH IN ADVERTISING AND PUBLIC RELATIONS

16 RESEARCH IN MEDIA EFFECTS

CHAPTER 13
Research in the Print Media

Although print media research, one of the first areas of mass communication research, first began in the 1920s, it is primarily since the 1950s that researchers have been applying quantitative research techniques to investigate mass media effects of newspapers and magazines.

Chapter 13 looks at the most common types of studies in newspaper and magazine research, with special emphasis on the research most likely to be conducted by advertiser-supported publications. Many of these methodologies are similar to those employed in other areas of research—content analysis, experiments, focus groups, and surveys. Print media research, however, tends to be more narrowly focused and more oriented toward practical application than is usually the case in other fields.

Research in the print media includes readership studies, which determine who reads a publication, what items are read, and why readers make the choices they do. Another common type of study is the circulation study, which examines penetration levels of newspapers and magazines as well as aspects of delivery and pricing systems.

Typography and makeup studies are concerned with the impact of various newspaper and magazine design elements on readership and item preferences. And, finally, readability studies investigate textual elements that affect message comprehension.

NAME _____

CLASS _____

DATE _____

<u>RESEARCH TERMS</u>

Use the space provided below to define the following terms.

1. Advertising exposure study (285)

2. Aided recall (289)

3. Basic market study (285)

4. Circulation research (295)

5. Cloze procedure (299)

6. Editor-reader comparison study (292)

7. Flesch reading ease formula (298)

8. Fog Index (299)

9. Item pretest (294)

10. Item-selection study (289)

11. Lifestyle segmentation research (288)

12. Readability (298)

13. Reader-nonreader study (290)

14. Reader panel (293)

15. Reader profile (288)

16. SMOG Grading (299)

17. Typography and makeup study (296)

18. Uses and gratifications study (291)

REVIEW QUESTIONS

Choose one response that best answers each question below.

1. Readership research became important to the management of newspapers and magazines from 1960-70 because of (288)

    a. increasingly well-known techniques for quantitative research
    b. the growing availability of basic research data
    c. competition with radio and television for advertising dollars
    d. declining circulation rates in metropolitan areas
    e. a and c are correct

2. An important factor in the acceptance by newspaper editors of research as vital to the industry was the (286)

    a. Newspaper Advertising Bureau
    b. Reader Interest Survey
    c. An increase in the number of articles on research published in scholarly journals
    d. The Newspaper Readership Project
    e. News Research Center

3. The most frequently used type of newspaper and magazine research is the (287)

    a. circulation study
    b. readership study
    c. typography study
    d. makeup study
    e. readability study

4. Researchers use which of the following to determine reader profiles? (288)

   a. studies that reflect demographics of populations
   b. studies that indicate what readers think and how they live
   c. studies that relate age to type of print media read
   d. studies that indicate items or categories read
   e. a and b are correct

5. Which of the following types of newspaper readership studies is used to determine motives? (291)

   a. reader-nonreader
   b. uses and gratifications
   c. reader profile
   d. item-selection
   e. editor-reader comparison

6. Psychographic studies provide information on (288)

   a. reader profiles
   b. differences in the nature and extent of reading
   c. levels of disagreement/agreement with attitudinal statements
   d. personal motivations and rewards
   e. a and c are correct

7. Data that result from psychographic studies are (288)

   a. compiled to determine psychological motivations
   b. used to differentiate readership interest among readers with similar demographic characteristics
   c. used to determine attitudes
   d. used to determine who reads specific magazines/newspapers
   e. b and c are correct

8. Researchers use the <u>item-selection study</u> (289)

    a. to reduce the expense required to conduct a uses and gratifications study
    b. to determine which sections of newspapers or magazines people read
    c. to find out what readers remember most about what they read on a daily basis
    d. as a substitute for "aided recall"
    e. to identify readers and nonreaders

9. An example of a <u>unit of analysis</u> in an item-selection study is (290)

    a. the entertainment page of a newspaper
    b. an article about declining birth rates
    c. all articles on interior design in a year
    d. the Sunday supplement
    e. a and b are correct

10. A national study indicates the most widely read newspaper stories are those concerned with (290)

    a. sports
    b. politics/economy
    c. disasters/tragedies
    d. lifestyle/entertainment
    e. human interest

11. A problem with using the <u>reader-nonreader study</u> is (290)

    a. it is difficult to isolate the variables to be analyzed
    b. it is difficult to operationally define a nonreader
    c. it often fails to measure what it was designed to measure
    d. the experimental focus is generally too restrictive
    e. a and b are correct

12. In newspaper research, <u>uses and gratifications studies</u> are designed to measure (291)

    a. motives
    b. psychological rewards
    c. reading patterns of ethnic groups
    d. decreasing readership
    e. a and b are correct

13. Which of the following is <u>most often named</u> as the strongest factor in explaining readership? (292)

    a. reading for information
    b. the need to keep up to date
    c. the need to be entertained
    d. the need to kill time
    e. the need for fun

14. Which of the following is <u>not</u> measured by an <u>editor-reader comparison study</u>? (293)

    a. reader preference for metropolitan newspapers
    b. articles a newspaper's staff believes are important
    c. reader likes and dislikes about a newspaper
    d. correspondence between reader and editor opinions
    e. perceptions about newspaper attributes

15. <u>Magazine readership studies</u> differ from research conducted for newspapers in that (293)

    a. the mail survey technique is more popular in magazine research
    b. they are generally more specific and focus on content
    c. most magazine articles are pretested and used as a guide for editorial decisions
    d. more money is spent annually on magazine research than newspaper research
    e. b and c are correct

16. Research that is conducted to measure <u>circulation</u> (296)

    a. determines circulation patterns in particular markets
    b. analyzes changes in newspaper buying patterns nationwide
    c. reveals that amounts of money spent promoting magazines is irrelevant to sales
    d. measures why people cancel their subscriptions
    e. a and d are correct

17. Which of the following research methods is used most often in <u>typography and makeup studies</u>? (296)

    a. focus groups
    b. mail surveys
    c. experimental method
    d. panel designs
    e. c and d are correct

18. <u>Readability tests</u> are designed to measure (298)

    a. educational level required for understanding a text
    b. reader interest in a piece of printed material
    c. layout as it relates to reader interest
    d. reader evaluation of content difficulty
    e. all of the above

19. Which of the following readability tests does <u>not</u> require a count of words or syllables? (299)

    a. SMOG Grading
    b. Cloze procedure
    c. Flesch reading ease formula
    d. Fog Index
    e. none of the above

20. <u>Readability research</u> reveals that overall (300)

    a. the readability of newspapers has become more difficult over the years
    b. magazines are easier to read than newspapers
    c. newspapers test at the 8th-grade reading level
    d. news stories are the most difficult to read
    e. readability formulas do not result in the same results when applied to magazines and newspapers

21. Surveys reveal that the type of research project conducted most often by magazines is the (301)

    a. telephone interview
    b. market study
    c. mail survey
    d. personal interview
    e. focus group

22. The most frequently conducted type of <u>newspaper</u> research study concerns (300)

    a. who is or is not a reader
    b. amount read
    c. circulation penetration
    d. what is read
    e. frequency of reading

RELATIONAL DEFINITIONS

In each example provided below, choose the <u>one</u> term or concept that does not fit with the others. Explain why.

1. readership/circulation/demographic/readability/typographic (287)

2. profile/demographic summary/lifestyle/attitudes/aided recall (288)

3. news article/feature story/crime news/psychographic characteristics (290)

4. staff/comparison/reader panel/journalist (292)

5. circulation research/item pretest/reader panel/mail survey (293)

6. market characteristics/typography/delivery systems/pricing (295)

7. Flesch/SMOG/Cloze/ANPA/Fog (298)

8. item selection/amount read/tabloid/selection of paper (301)

9. market study/reader profile/editorial articles/reader traffic studies (302)

CONCEPT APPLICATION QUESTIONS

1. Research in the print media (in comparison to other areas of mass media research) is described as "narrowly focused and...oriented toward practical application." Provide an example of a type of research question that could be used for both newspapers and magazines (as opposed to a study of broadcast media) that would illustrate why this is so.

2. You have been the owner of the only newspaper in a small Ohio town for many years. A recent college graduate has decided to begin another newspaper that will compete with yours. Which type of readership study would you be most likely to use to determine how to keep your current subscription level? Explain your choice.

3. The publisher of a widely circulated newspaper wants to reduce costs or the paper will likely go out of business. To prevent this from happening, the publisher has decided to eliminate some of the paper's coverage. Describe a research study that would be applicable to determine which section(s) of the paper is (are) most expendable. Name a unit of analysis that could be used for each section.

4. Two years ago you began publishing a magazine for business men and women ages 22-30. Initially, the magazine was a huge success, but circulation has been falling off in the past 6 months. How could you determine what changes need to be made in the magazine to recapture your readers' interest?

CHAPTER 14
Research in the Electronic Media

The value of mass media research has increased dramatically in the period of time between the 1930s when radio became a popular medium, until today, when the success or failure of the radio and television industry depends on knowing the who's, why's, and how's of audiences. Because commercial broadcasting is primarily supported by advertising, it is vital that broadcasters and advertisers have information about the continually shifting demographics, characteristics, and likes and dislikes of their audiences.

Electronic media research falls into two major categories: ratings and nonratings research. <u>Ratings research</u> generally relates to syndicated data collected by such companies as the Arbitron Ratings Company, the A. C. Nielsen Company, and Birch Radio. <u>Nonratings research</u> encompasses all other types of quantitative and qualitative research used by broadcasters.

The purpose of Chapter 14 is to provide an introduction to research in radio, television, and cable. The chapter provides a basic understanding of the type of work conducted by electronic media researchers and is intended to offer a stepping-stone for understanding more sophisticated methodologies and topics discussed in advanced qualitative and quantitative research texts.

NAME   _____

CLASS _____

DATE   _____

RESEARCH TERMS

Use the space provided below to define the following terms.

1. Adjacent ADI (319)

2. Area of dominant influence (ADI) (319)

3. Audience rating (316)

4. Audience share (317)

5. Audience turnover (321)

6. Audimeter (SIA) (311)

7. Auditorium music test (332)

8. Average quarter-hour (AQH) (321)

9. BehaviorScan (331)

10. Call-out research (332)

11. Cost per thousand (CPM) (318)

12. Cume (321)

13. Daypart (321)

14. Diary (311)

15. Expanded Sample Frame (310)

16. Gross rating points (GRP) (321)

17. Homes using television (HUT) (316)

18. Hook (332)

19. Metro area survey (MSA) (319)

20. Multistage area probability sampling (310)

21. National Audience Composition (NAC) (308)

22. National Station Index (NSI) (308)

23. National Television Index (NTI) (308)

24. Overnights (309)

25. People meters (327)

26. Performer Q (334)

27. Persons using radio (PUR) (316)

28. Program Appeal Index (328)

29. Program Impact Index (329)

30. Radio's All-Dimension Audience Research (RADAR) (309)

31. Randomization of Last Digits (310)

32. Reach (321)

33. Rough cut (330)

34. ScanAmerica (327)

35. Sweeps (309)

36. Telephone coincidental (314)

37. Television meter (TVM) (311)

38. Testsight (331)

39. Total survey area (TSA) (319)

40. Total Telephone Frame (310)

REVIEW QUESTIONS

Choose **one** response that **best** answers each question below.

1. The most significant factor in the development of <u>electronic mass media research</u> was (307)

    a. broadcast signal problems
    b. television
    c. government media-subsidy policies
    d. advertising
    e. none of the above

2. The area of media research referred to as psychographics analyzes (308)

   a. audience size
   b. message effectiveness
   c. lifestyle patterns
   d. people's behavior
   e. c and d are correct

3. Which of the following research companies conducts local market ratings? (308)

   a. Birch Radio
   b. Arbitron Ratings Company
   c. A. C. Nielsen
   d. Dun and Bradstreet
   e. a and b are correct

4. The only network television ratings service in the country is (308)

   a. National Station Index (NSI)
   b. National Audience Composition (NAC)
   c. National Television Index (NIT)
   d. RADAR
   e. a and c are correct

5. Sweeps are conducted in which of the following time periods? (309)

   a. January, March, August, November
   b. March, June, September, December
   c. February, April, August, October
   d. February, May, July, November
   e. December, March, June, October

6. Overnights are defined as (309)

   a. ratings data gathered by electronic meters
   b. preliminary ratings data of a previous night's programs
   c. a combination of sample data from the day a program is aired plus two days
   d. local market radio and TV data of a previous night's programming
   e. a and b are correct

7. The largest <u>ratings</u> company in the United States that collects radio-audience listening estimates is (309)

    a. A. C. Nielsen
    b. Arbitron Ratings Company
    c. Statistical Research, Inc.
    d. Control Data Corporation
    e. b and c are correct

8. <u>Ratings</u> measure (309)

    a. parameters of audience size
    b. opinions
    c. facts about audiences
    d. estimates of audience size
    e. a and b are correct

9. Which of the following is <u>not</u> used to gather data for ratings surveys? (310)

    a. telephone interviews
    b. electronic recordings
    c. door-to-door interviews
    d. diaries
    e. audimeters

10. <u>Multistage area probability sampling</u> is used to (310)

    a. sample diverse populations
    b. conduct a census of media usage
    c. reflect actual population distributions
    d. gather network TV ratings
    e. c and d are correct

11. A <u>drawback</u> of using the audimeter to collect ratings data is (313)

    a. low return from minority groups
    b. inaccuracy of data collection
    c. the inability to record the number of people watching per household
    d. samples do not reflect actual population distributions
    e. the inability to record channel switchings

12. The procedure <u>telephone coincidental</u> refers to (314)

    a. conducting custom survey research
    b. calling households the day after a program has aired
    c. measuring the size of an audience for a given time period
    d. reporting start and stop times of listening periods
    e. a and c are correct

13. To determine an <u>audience rating</u>, researchers must know which of the following? (316)

    a. number of persons per household
    b. percentage of households in a population
    c. combined ratings of all stations during a specific time period
    d. percentage of persons tuned to a specific channel or network
    e. b and d are correct

14. The term <u>cost per thousand</u> refers to (318)

    a. a way to assess the efficiency of advertising
    b. a way to assess the effectiveness of a commercial message
    c. a dollar estimate of an ad's reach
    d. the amount it costs to survey 1,000 households
    e. a and c are correct

15. The <u>total survey area</u> defines (319)

    a. metro survey area
    b. designated market areas
    c. area of dominant influence
    d. a market's adjacent reach
    e. all of the above

16. The term <u>unduplicated audience</u> refers to which of the following? (321)

    a. persons who listen at least 5 minutes within a given daypart
    b. a daypart
    c. an average quarter hour
    d. persons tuned to a specific channel for at least 5 minutes in a 15-minute time segment
    e. b and d are correct

17. <u>Gross rating points</u> are determined by totaling (321)

    a. the average quarter hour and the cumulative audience
    b. a station's ratings during 2 or more dayparts
    c. a station's rating for a period of a week
    d. audience turnover plus cume
    e. none of the above

18. Which of the following must be considered before ratings can be <u>interpreted</u>? (325)

    a. whether or not ratings must be weighted
    b. undersampled age/sex groups
    c. rate of error
    d. population estimates
    e. a and c are correct

19. <u>People meters</u>, as opposed to traditional TV meters, indicate (327)

    a. how many people per household are watching TV
    b. which channel a TV set is tuned to
    c. the number of visitors in a household who are watching TV
    d. the effects of exposure to commercials
    e. all of the above

20. An anticipated <u>problem</u> with the continued use of people meters is (328)

    a. accuracy of data collection
    b. sample turnover
    c. the quality of sample selected
    d. mechanical difficulties
    e. b and c are correct

21. <u>Nonratings research</u> provides data about which of the following? (329)

    a. audience size
    b. audience likes and dislikes
    c. audience composition
    d. different types of programs
    e. b and d are correct

RELATIONAL DEFINITIONS

In each example provided below, choose the one term or concept that does not fit with the others. Explain why.

1. metered markets/A. C. Nielsen/preliminary ratings data/diary (309)

2. electronic recordings/telephone interviews/surveys/diaries (310)

3. national census data/NTI/population distributions/telephone coincidental (310)

4. SIA/Arbitron/audimeter/sample data (311)

5. audience size/telephone/custom research studies/share (314)

6. percent of people/percent of HH/percent of PUR/specific station (316)

7. prime time/ratings book/broadcast day/CPM (316)

CONCEPT APPLICATION QUESTIONS

1. Assume that Nielsen has gathered the following sample data from a total population of 90 million television HHs viewing network TV Monday-Friday from 12:00-3:00 p.m.

Network	HHs Viewing
ABC	300
CBS	450
NBC	350
Not watching	700

   Using the above data, determine the following:

   a. Each network's rating

   ABC _____
   CBS _____
   NBC _____

   b. Each network's share

   ABC _____
   CBS _____
   NBC _____

   c. Sample HUT   _____

   d. Population HUT   _____

   e. HH estimates for each network

   ABC _____
   CBS _____
   NBC _____

2. Company Y wants to purchase advertising on NBC during a soap opera that airs from 1:00-2:00 p.m. Assume the cost for a 30-second spot is $200,000. Using the information from Question 5 determine the CPM.

3. Referring to the sample page from an Aribitron ratings book (Figure 14.3, page 320 of your text), determine the following:

   a. WGNX's ADI rating and share for daypart 7:30P-8:00P.

      Rating _____

      Share _____

   b. Which station wins the ADI 8:00P-11:00P daypart?

      _____

   c. In number of share points, what is the difference in WSB's performance from February 1984 to February 1985 in the 6:00P-8:00P daypart?

      _____

   d. The estimated number of TSA women aged 25-49 who watched WXIA Monday-Friday in the 11:00P-11:30P daypart.

      _____

   e. Calculate with data from columns 18-23 the estimated women aged 35-49 watching WSB Monday-Friday in the 6:00P-7:30P daypart.

      _____

4. Again referring to the Arbitron sample page on 320 of your text, answer the following:

   a. Company X is opening a new store in the inner city and wants to purchase commercial time on station WAGA, Monday-Friday from 6:00-7:30 p.m. to promote the opening. Which data will be most significant for them to consider? Why?

   b. Company Z is introducing a new line of men's cologne and wants to purchase commercial time on Monday-Friday from 6:00-8:00 p.m. to target men aged 18-34. Which station would be most advantageous for them to consider? Why?

5. Referring to sample AQH and cume data (Figure 14.4, page 323 of your text), determine the following:

   a. The estimated number of metro adults aged 18-49 listening to WMMR _____

   b. The metro adult cume audience over 18 years old listening to station WPST _____

   c. WCAU's turnover for adults over 18 years old _____

   d. The metro station with the lowest share for adults aged 25-54 _____

   e. The station on which you would likely advertise if you were a real estate agent for a retirement village _____

   f. The total cume audience for ages 25-49 _____

6. If a random sample of 2,000 households produces a rating of 40, what would be the standard error? What then is the actual range for the rating?

   Standard error _____

   Rating range _____

7. Population estimates show that in a particular area 35,250 men aged 20-24 account for 7.2% of the population. A researcher distributed a total of 1,000 diaries to a sample of this population. Ten of the male viewers in the audience did not return them. How must the data be weighted to adjust for this deficiency?

8. In what ways does the kind of information provided by nonratings research differ from that gathered by ratings research?

9. A production company has developed a commercial for a new outdoor cafe soon to open in Sacramento. Name two methods a researcher might use to determine the effectiveness of the commercial before it is aired on local television. Once the commercial has aired, name two postproduction research methods that could be used.

10. Researchers are often asked to determine listener acceptance of a radio station's music programming. Describe the two most widely used methods of testing a station's playlist.

CHAPTER 15
Research in Advertising and Public Relations

Increased competition, mass markets, and mounting costs have given impetus to the increased use of research as a basic management tool in the advertising and public relations industries.

Chapter 15 discusses the more common areas of _advertising_ and _public relations research_ and the types of studies they entail. Research in these industries involves most of the methods discussed in earlier chapters--laboratory, survey, field research, and content analysis, among others--adapted to provide specific types of information that meet the needs of these industries. However, most research in advertising and public relations is oriented toward solving specific problems and, unlike other areas discussed so far in this course, is not concerned with theorizing or generalizing to other situations.

The three fundamental research areas of advertising discussed in depth in this chapter include: _copy research_, _media research_, and _campaign assessment research_.

Copy testing consists of studies that examine a particular advertisement or commercial. _Media research_ helps determine which advertising vehicles are the most efficient and what type of media schedule will have the greatest impact. _Campaign assessment studies_ examine the overall response of consumers to an advertising campaign.

Research in _public relations_ includes monitoring relevant developments and trends, studying the public relations position of an organization, examining the messages produced by an organization, and measuring how well an organization is living up to its social responsibilities, as well as evaluating public relations campaigns.

RESEARCH TERMS

Use the space provided below to define the following terms.

1. Aided recall (344)

2. Applied research (342)

3. Circulation (352)

4. Cognitive dimension (344)

5. Communication audit (366)

6. Copy testing (343)

7. Dimensions of impact (343)

8. Environmental monitoring programs (364)

9. Evaluation research (366)

10. Forced exposure (348)

11. Frequency (351)

12. Galvanic skin response (349)

13. Masked recall (353)

14. Media efficiency (354)

15. Message research (343)

16. Public relations audit (365)

17. Pupillometer test (349)

18. Reach (351)

19. Reader traffic score (344)

20. Recall study (344)

21. Recognition (353)

22. Rough cut (343)

23. Social audit (366)

24. Stepwise analysis (355)

25. Tracking studies (361)

26. Unaided recall technique (344)

REVIEW QUESTIONS

Choose <u>one</u> response that <u>best</u> answers each question below.

1. In <u>copy testing</u>, researchers focus primarily on which of the following? (343)

    a. how layout and design determine ad effectiveness
    b. how ads use text to structure ideas
    c. comparing the variables in an ad for effectiveness
    d. comparing the effectiveness of one or more ads
    e. c and d are correct

2. Another name for <u>copy testing research</u> is (343)

    a. advertising stimulus measurement
    b. message research
    c. advertising research
    d. applied research
    e. a and b are correct

3. The <u>overall</u> goal of copy testing research is to (343)

    a. determine the most effective content of an ad before the ad is completed
    b. determine how ad recall is affected by variations in an ad
    c. test for readability and recall
    d. define the purpose or goal of an ad
    e. a and b are correct

4. Which of the following is <u>not</u> considered a <u>dimension of impact</u> in the persuasion process? (343)

    a. knowing
    b. doing
    c. feeling
    d. believing
    e. none of the above

5. Key dependent variables of the cognitive dimension of impact do not include (344)

   a. attention
   b. awareness
   c. involvement
   d. comprehension
   e. recall

6. A reader traffic score is compiled with (344)

   a. cognitive dimension variables
   b. data about what subjects recall seeing or reading
   c. panel study reactions to a series of ads
   d. respondent-remembered lists of advertisers
   e. a and b are correct

7. As recall studies, telephone surveys are most commonly used to test the effectiveness of (344)

   a. newspaper ads
   b. radio commercials
   c. magazine ads
   d. TV commercials
   e. b and d are correct

8. The unaided recall technique enables researchers to (344)

   a. force respondents to describe specific ads
   b. force respondents to choose a memorable ad
   c. identify respondent recall of brand names
   d. eliminate respondent's desire to please the researcher
   e. a and b are correct

9. The term "Burkes" with regard to recall tests means (345)

   a. commercials tested by Burke Marketing Research
   b. average ad recall scores
   c. percentage of respondents who recall seeing a particular advertisement
   d. degree of favorable attitude toward a product in an ad
   e. positive statements made by respondents about ads

10. Recall studies are <u>not</u> designed to measure (346)

    a. ad recognition
    b. purchasing behavior
    c. ad effectiveness
    d. percentage of favorable or unfavorable comments
    e. a and b are correct

11. The <u>affective dimension</u> in advertising research refers to (346)

    a. comprehension of ad content
    b. change in degree of like of dislike for a product
    c. likelihood of purchasing brand products
    d. one's feelings about a particular ad
    e. changes in buying preference

12. Which of the following is most commonly used to measure <u>attitude change</u> about ads? (348)

    a. buying intention scale
    b. semantic differential
    c. rating scale
    d. index
    e. b and c are correct

13. To determine whether an ad has <u>changed</u> a consumer's attitude about a product, a research test must (348)

    a. reveal the consumer's satisfaction with the product
    b. reveal the consumer's attitude before a purchase
    c. reveal the consumer's attitude after reviewing an ad
    d. measure the amount of time between exposure to an ad and attitude change, if any
    e. a and c are correct

14. The <u>forced-exposure</u> method of testing consumer attitudes (348)

    a. is used only in radio ad recall
    b. asks respondents to complete attitudinal questionnaires about products
    c. exposes respondents to TV shows and ads about specific products
    d. tests how respondents change their evaluations
    e. b and d are correct

15. The <u>conative dimension</u> of advertising research deals with (349)

    a. how respondents interpret ad content
    b. the underlying theme respondents assign to ad campaigns
    c. what respondents buy as a result of being exposed to an ad
    d. how respondents switch brands after viewing an ad for a product
    e. c and d are correct

16. To determine <u>buying preferences</u>, researchers (350)

    a. measure customer recall of a product against subsequent buying of that product
    b. count the number of coupons returned to a retailer
    c. watch people shop
    d. take periodic store inventories
    e. all of the above

17. When a message's <u>reach</u> increases, the average frequency of the message can be expected to (351)

    a. remain about the same
    b. decrease
    c. increase
    d. double
    e. increase 1.5 times

18. The <u>most commonly used</u> advertising studies in print and electronic media research concern (352)

    a. exposure length and number
    b. circulation data
    c. market size
    d. audience analysis
    e. reach and frequency

19. Audience size of a newspaper is measured in terms of (352)

    a. paid subscriptions
    b. total copies sold per edition
    c. number of readers versus nonreaders
    d. number of copies sold annually
    e. percentage of increase or decrease during a 6-month period

20. An audience size study designed to measure the average number of readers of a particular publication uses the technique of (353)

    a. asking respondents if they have subscribed to a magazine or newspaper within a specified period of time
    b. asking respondents to specify magazines or newspapers they have read in a particular period of time
    c. giving respondents names of newspapers and magazines and asking them if they have read them in a particular period of time
    d. asking respondents to recall previously published ads
    e. b and c are correct

21. Variables that cannot be considered when determining the media efficiency of an ad include (354)

    a. readers per issue
    b. number of ad exposures per issue
    c. circulation
    d. audience composition
    e. style of advertisement

22. Researchers use which of the following to determine the effects of ad exposure via several advertising vehicles simultaneously? (355)

    a. targeting easiest-to-reach customers first
    b. computing probable sales responses for each market segment
    c. calculating the probability that someone in a particular market segment will be exposed to an ad
    d. maximizing favorable attitude changes toward an advertised product
    e. all of the above

RELATIONAL DEFINITIONS

In each example provided below, choose the <u>one</u> term or concept that does not fit with the others. Explain why.

1. commercial/pretest/posttest/cognitive (342)

2. exposure/comprehension/recall/attitude change (344)

3. tracking study/nonreader/associated reader/noted reader (346)

4. measure/sales/direct response/redeemable coupons (349)

5. frequency/total households/4 weeks/cumulative audience (351)

6. aided recall/recognition/CPM/unaided recall (353)

7. stepwise analysis/decision calculus/objective function/media efficiency (355)

8. number of exposures/household/same message/gross rating points (351)

247

CONCEPT APPLICATION QUESTIONS

1. An ad agency has created an advertising campaign for a new type of bubble gum that will not get hard no matter how long it is chewed. Your client wants to use the copy-testing method to determine the effectiveness of your ads before they are aired on television. Describe an appropriate research method a researcher might use for each of the three dimensions of impact in the persuasion process.

2. In a city of 60,000 residents, 6,000 households have been sent a flyer advertising a new car wash in the city. The frequency for the sample of households is 18,000. Determine the reach and the average frequency of the advertising message.

3. Handsome Hal wants to place a personal ad in either the Daily Chatterbox, which charges $100 for a personal ad and has a circulation of 5,000, or in the Weekly Tattletale, which sells the same size advertising space for $50 but is purchased by 8,000 readers.

   a. By determining the CPM, decide in which newspaper Handsome Hal should place his ad.

   b. How could a researcher determine the total audience size for Handsome Hal's ad?

4. As a researcher, you have been asked to pretest and posttest a newspaper ad for volunteer help in a community fund-raising event to provide shelter for the homeless. What variables might you study in a recall test to determine the effectiveness of the ad after it has been published?

5. A manufacturer wants to begin an advertising campaign for blue suede shoes and can choose to advertise in either a magazine with a reach of 20% and an average frequency of 2.5 or in another magazine that has a reach of 40% and a average frequency of 1.0. Which would be the better buy? Explain.

CHAPTER 16
Research in Media Effects

While the three preceding chapters have focused on research conducted in professional or industrial settings, a great deal of mass media research is conducted at colleges and universities.

Academic and private-sector research share common techniques in the effort to predict and explain behavior. But academic research differs from private-sector research in that the former is public, more theoretical in nature, generally determined more by the individual researcher than by management, and usually less costly than private-sector research.

Chapter 16 looks at examples of the more popular types of research conducted by academic researchers and shows how this work relates to private-sector research.

Presented in this chapter is an overview of the history, methods, and theoretical development of five research areas that exemplify scholarly mass media research: (1) the antisocial and prosocial effects of specific media content, (2) uses and gratifications, (3) agenda setting, (4) cultivation of perceptions of social reality, and (5) advertising and the socialization of children.

RESEARCH TERMS

Use the space provided below to define the following terms.

1. Agenda setting theory (385)

2. Antisocial effects (372)

3. Catharsis approach (379)

4. Desensitization (380)

5. Minimal effects position (373)

6. Prosocial content (373)

7. Social learning theory (380)

8. Stimulation theory (379)

9. Theory of media effects (373)

REVIEW QUESTIONS

Choose **one** response below that **best** answers each question.

1. Generally, it can be said that <u>academic mass media research</u> (372)

    a. is concerned with how the real world can apply theoretical knowledge about mass media effects
    b. generates data that is useful to the private sector in understanding the effects of mass media
    c. develops techniques and research approaches to be used by the private sector
    d. is oriented toward developing theories of mass media
    e. is concerned with social impact issues of mass media

2. The most <u>heavily</u> researched area in mass media concerns (372)

    a. perceptions of social reality
    b. advertising and the socialization of children
    c. why people engage in various forms of media behavior
    d. the relationship between media and audience priorities in the importance of news topics
    e. antisocial effects of media content

3. The <u>minimal effects</u> position regarding media concerns (373)

    a. the degree of antisocial effects that result from mass communication
    b. how media reinforce existing attitudes and predispositions
    c. the impact of prosocial content on media users
    d. the idea that in reality, the media do not change people's beliefs and attitudes
    e. b and d are correct

4. Researchers generally agree that with regard to the social effects of mass media (374)

   a. violence is linked with television viewing
   b. society is more negatively affected by motion picture viewing than positively
   c. TV violence is related to antisocial behaviors among juvenile viewers
   d. there is no conclusive evidence of a cause-and-effect relationship between TV viewing and subsequent imitation of antisocial behavior
   e. there is a relationship between prosocial TV programs and prosocial behavior among children

5. The research technique that has shown the strongest positive relationship between viewing media violence and aggression is (379)

   a. a panel study
   b. a field experiment
   c. a laboratory experiment
   d. a survey
   e. b and c are correct

6. The catharsis approach in the controversy over the impact of media violence suggests that (379)

   a. repeated exposure to media violence results in little change in the level of aggressive behavior
   b. aggressive urges are purged as a result of viewing fantasy expressions of hostility
   c. viewing violence prompts more aggression on the part of the viewer
   d. a lessening of aggressive behavior is more often than not the case after children view violent content
   e. b and d are correct

7. Which concept listed below suggests that people who are heavily exposed to violence and antisocial acts become less anxious about the consequences? (380)

   a. stimulation theory
   b. uses and gratifications
   c. desensitization
   d. excitation transfer
   e. assimilation

8. Which of the following is not a factor in the performance of antisocial acts after exposure to aggression? (380)

   a. the degree of reinforcement or punishment that accompanies performance of the observed behavior
   b. the degree to which the media behavior is perceived to be real
   c. the length of time a subject is exposed to aggression
   d. the emotional arousal of the subjects
   e. the presence of cues in the postobservation environment

9. The research approach used to determine why people become engaged in various forms of media behavior is referred to as (381)

   a. stimulation theory
   b. uses and gratification
   c. enculturation
   d. catharsis
   e. cultivation

10. The type of research that examines the relationship between media and audience priorities is referred to as (385)

    a. content analytic
    b. impact theory
    c. agenda setting
    d. paired comparison
    e. grouping theory

11. Agenda setting theory proposes that (385)

    a. populations determine the direction and content of news
    b. media influence which public issues are important
    c. media are usually successful in determining what people value
    d. media news has minimal impact on public awareness of issues
    e. b and c are correct

12. Researchers have found that public agendas are difficult to define because (387)

    a. respondents are not equally aware of public issues
    b. the effect of time on formation of media agenda is unknown
    c. it is difficult to determine the difference between a respondent's intra- and interpersonal agendas
    d. it is impossible to determine the duration of an audience's agenda
    e. all of the above are correct

13. The basis assumption of <u>enculturation research</u> is that (389)

    a. if media are the main source of information, audience perceptions will be influenced in the direction of the media portrayal
    b. there is no conclusive evidence that viewer perceptions of reality are affected by the media
    c. paranoia and predisposition to aggressive behavior is directly related to amount of time spent watching TV
    d. the more audiences are exposed to media portrayals and themes, the more their perceptions concur with the media
    e. c and d are correct

14. If the Action for Children's Television recommendations concerning commercials on children's programs had become reality, (394)

    a. celebrities would have been banned as spokespersons
    b. commercials would be banned during the hours of the day when children would most likely watch TV
    c. commercials would be banned from all children's programs
    d. commercials for food products would be banned
    e. commercials for toys deemed violent would be banned

15. Studies indicate which of the following is a <u>crucial</u> variable in determining children's understanding of TV advertising? (394)

    a. level of intelligence
    b. socioeconomic level
    c. age
    d. content of the advertisement
    e. a and c are correct

RELATIONAL DEFINITIONS

In each example provided below, choose the <u>one</u> term or concept that does not fit with the others. Explain why.

1. social effects/uses and gratifications/agenda setting/enculturation (372)

2. catharsis/stimulation/retention/desensitization (379)

3. Joseph Klapper/George Gerbner/Bruce Springsteen/Al Bandura (373)

4. excitation transfer/media-induced arousal/interpersonal behavior/social learning theory (380)

5. traditional effects approach/consumption behaviors/social variables/media behavior (381)

6. intrapersonal agenda/rating issues/paired comparison/media agenda (387)

7. influenced perceptions/repeated exposures/cognitive development theory/enculturation (389)

CONCEPT APPLICATION QUESTIONS

1. The producer of a local television talk show has asked you to participate in a panel discussion on the relationship between viewing media violence and children's aggressive behavior. Based on research in this area, what information might you give to support the argument that children learn violent behavior from watching television and movies?

2. In what ways could a radio advertising salesperson use the findings generated from uses and gratifications research to sell advertising time to local merchants?

3. How does a significant historical and media event such as the explosion of the Challenger shuttle in January 1986 illustrate the agenda setting theory?

4. Negative political advertising became commonplace during the 1986 election year. Using the cultivation theory as the basis for your answer, what effect do you think these types of commercials had on voter perception of candidates and voting behavior?

5. Atkin (see page 397 of your text) found that children heavily exposed to Saturday morning commercials argued more with their parents when requests for an advertised product were turned down than did light viewers. Based on what you have read about advertising and the socialization of children, how might these findings be explained?

PART FIVE
Analyzing and Reporting Data

17 THE COMPUTER AS A RESEARCH TOOL

18 RESEARCH REPORTING, ETHICS, AND FINANCIAL SUPPORT

CHAPTER 17
The Computer as a Research Tool

As a result of the introduction of microcomputers in the early 1980s, the field of mass media research has been literally reshaped. Because it is now possible to conduct even the most sophisticated research using a computer that costs only several thousand dollars, it is extremely important that anyone interested in mass media research have a basic understanding of how computers, particularly microcomputers, are used.

Chapter 17 serves as an introduction to computers, with an emphasis on microcomputers. Beginning researchers must first become familiar with basic computer terminology as well as the language and acronyms associated with computer hardware and software. As a result, this chapter focuses on common definitions associated with basic computer technology and does not include Review Questions, Relational Definitions, or Concept Application Questions.

RESEARCH TERMS

Use the space provided below to define the following terms.

1. ASCII (413)

2. Batch processing (410)

3. Baud rate (416)

4. Bit (413)

5. Buffer (414)

6. CPU (412)

7. Data base (410)

8. Disk drive (413)

9. DOS (414)

10. Download (410)

11. Floppy disk (414)

12. Format (414)

13. Hard disk (414)

14. Hardware (412)

15. K (413)

16. Modem (415)

17. Monitor (415)

18. OCR (412)

19. Peripheral (412)

20. PROM (413)

21. RAM (413)

22. ROM (413)

23. Software (416)

24. Spreadsheet (419)

25. Time sharing (410)

CHAPTER 18
Research Reporting, Ethics, and Financial Support

Knowing how, why, and when to conduct mass media research has been the primary focus of the text. However, also important to the execution of any research project are the principles involved in the actual writing of the final research report, questions of ethics and research, and the underpinnings of necessary financial support.

Chapter 18 focuses on the steps involved in preparing a research report, including determining the appropriate organization, style, and mode of presentation suited to a specific audience.

Ethical questions are particularly important in mass media research since such research involves observations of human beings. It goes without saying that researchers must make every attempt to protect the rights, values, and decisions of participants in research studies. The chapter discusses guidelines designed to increase researcher awareness and sensitivity to ethical issues.

Finally, the chapter discusses a variety of sources as well as some of the problems involved with finding the financial support necessary to conduct mass media research.

Because this chapter is concerned with practical and philosophical issues related to mass media research, we have omitted sections on Research Terms, Relational Definitions, and Review Questions, and have concentrated only on Concept Application Questions.

CONCEPT APPLICATION QUESTIONS

1. Referring to page 432 of your text, describe the breach of ethics illustrated in each of the five hypothetical research situations presented, and explain how each example might be corrected.

2. As editor of a scholarly mass media research journal, you have been asked to speak to a beginning research class on how to prepare a research report for publication in your journal. List the most important points you will discuss with the students.

3. A researcher recruits 50 college students to be volunteers in a study to measure speed and accuracy of completion of basic statistical problems. The researcher instructs the students to do their own work and states that the study will be conducted on the "honor system." The first ten students who complete the study will receive $50 each. After completing the instructions, the researcher leaves the room and goes to an adjoining room with a two-way mirror where the students can be observed without their knowledge. Is this situation an example of concealment or deception? Explain your answer.

DATE DUE
